The
DIGITAL MOM
HANDBOOK

The
DIGITAL MOM HANDBOOK

How to Blog, Vlog, Tweet, and Facebook
Your Way to a Dream Career at Home

AUDREY McCLELLAND AND **COLLEEN PADILLA**

HARPER
BUSINESS

NEW YORK · LONDON · TORONTO · SYDNEY

HARPER
BUSINESS

All photographs courtesy of the authors.

This book is written as a source of information only. The information contained in this book should by no means be considered a substitute for the advice, decisions, or judgment of the reader's lawyer's, accountants, or other professional advisors.

All efforts have been made to ensure the accuracy of information as of the date published. The author and the publisher expressly disclaim responsibility for any adverse effects arising from the use or application of the information contained herein.

THE DIGITAL MOM HANDBOOK. Copyright © 2011 by Audrey McClelland and Colleen Padilla. All rights reserved. Printed in the United States of America. No part of this book may be used or reproduced in any manner whatsoever without written permission except in the case of brief quotations embodied in critical articles and reviews. For information address HarperCollins Publishers, 10 East 53rd Street, New York, NY 10022.

HarperCollins books may be purchased for educational, business, or sales promotional use. For information please write: Special Markets Department, Harper-Collins Publishers, 10 East 53rd Street, New York, NY 10022.

FIRST EDITION

Designed by Aline C. Pace & Tamara E. Jerardo

Library of Congress Cataloging-in-Publication Data

McClelland, Audrey Couto.
   The digital mom handbook : how to blog, vlog, tweet, and facebook your way to a dream career at home / Audrey McClelland and Colleen Padilla.
      p. cm.
   ISBN 978-0-06-204827-1 (pbk.)
   1. Working mothers—United States. 2. Home-based businesses—United States. 3. Child rearing—Economic aspects—United States. 4. Self-employed women—United States. 5. Women—Computer network resources. 6. Electronic commerce. 7. Telecommuting. 8. Internet. I. Padilla, Colleen. II. Title.
   HQ759.48.M374 2011
   658'.04120973—dc22
                                    2011007065

11 12 13 14 15   OV/RRD   10 9 8 7 6 5 4 3 2

To all the Digital Moms and all the Digital Moms-to-be.

Contents

A Letter to Our Readers

Dear Readers:

Mothers have been looking for the middle ground for more than half a century. Staying at home and raising the kids full time isn't it. Working full time and rushing home to tuck the kids in at 7 p.m. sharp ain't it, either. Even part-time work outside the house can be a scramble for most women as they try to "have it all" between 9 a.m. and 5 p.m. To work or not to work? That seems to be the bottom-line question for most women today.

But we believe that equation is changing. In fact, we're living proof of that change.

Both of us left the corporate ladder behind to stay home with our children. But instead of assigning us permanent stay-at-home status, this choice was the catalyst to our reinvention. Miles apart, we sat down at our computers one day, kids cooing in the background, and began to blog. Colleen specialized in product reviews; her blog was called ClassyMommy.com. Audrey was a down-to-earth fashionista who'd once landed a dream job with Donna Karan; her site, MomGenerations.com, focused on fashion trends for moms. Slowly but surely, our audiences grew. The portability of computers and smartphones, the connective powers of social networks, and an overwhelming desire to happily mix work and family enabled us to move past the Mommy Wars (i.e., stay-at-home moms vs. working moms) into a territory all our own. Today we are bona fide online entrepreneurs; our respective blogs lure upward of 200,000-plus viewers a month; we've been quoted by *Good Morning America,* Fox News, ABC News, even the *New York Times;* and we've forged alliances with the biggest corporations around, including Frigidaire, Tide, T.J.Maxx, and Hanes (they call *us* for advice about their products—and they listen!).

We're telling you all this not because we enjoy tooting our own horns but because writing it down makes it real for us. And we honestly believe that other moms can do the same. After all, neither of us even knew how to create a blog when we started out! What we did know, though, was that we wanted a change, so we dove in and began blogging, tweeting, skyping, vlogging, and facebooking. Four years later, our lives as moms will never be the same.

We may not be the fashion designers, corporate execs, or journalists we once aspired to be. However, we're something we think is even more fun—something that lets us balance our mommyhood with our sanity.

Most days, we can sit on a play-mat beside our children, a sippy cup in one hand and an iPhone in the other, and get motherhood and "career-hood" taken care of. Thanks to the endless possibilities on the Internet, we've found the magical middle ground. We each defined the terms "career" and "success" for ourselves—no person or corporation did it for us.

Not bad for a day's work.

The Digital Mom Handbook is our attempt to show other moms how to find their own middle ground via the frontier of the Internet. Do you want to be a booming six-figure eBay saleswoman? A twenty-hour-a-week brand consultant? A local Twitter correspondent? The terms are yours to define. Money, hours-per-week, title—these don't dictate your Digital Mom success. Personal satisfaction does. That's a very important takeaway, and we'll repeat it often.

Over the course of this book, we'll share our stories, as well as those of other moms who have found success online. Ultimately, though, becoming a Digital Mom is a highly personal journey. The reasons why we started won't be the reasons why you start—except perhaps to make a bit more money, because everyone could use that—and that's okay. The last thing we want is to tell you that your online experience needs to be identical to ours. After all, what fun would that be? You might not be interested in fashion or product reviews at all. Maybe you'll even come up with a better way to launch your blog than we did.

Instead, we'll try to give you all the tools and advice you'll need—tools and advice we wish we'd had when we were starting out!—to have your own successful Digital Mom experience. And the most important part of getting started is figuring out what it is that you really want to write about, so in our first chapter we'll help you find your own passion.

Whether your passion is geography or politics or food or the geopolitics of food, you're about to start a project that will change your life—by design. We hope you enjoy every second of it!

Digitally yours,

Audrey and Colleen

The
DIGITAL MOM
HANDBOOK

Introduction

 Our Stories

Technologies that let us balance the competing demands of family, housework, paid labor, and the responsibilities of being the social glue in many relationships are technologies that women have in their lives. It is perhaps unsurprising, against that backdrop, that women also find themselves gravitating to social media and social networking tools. Facebook, Twitter, and other online community sites can fit into and support our fragmented lives and fulfill our need to connect with others, regardless of time or distance.

—Dr. Genevieve Bell, cultural anthropologist, Intel fellow, and Intel Labs Director, Interaction and Experience Research

Technology and blogging have truly changed our lives. We both never imagined that someday when someone asked us what we did for a living, we'd say, "I blog." More likely we would have said, "We travel to the moon!" But one thing we've learned about the social media world: the sky is the limit. We both started blogging for very different reasons, and we each have our own distinct story. We want to give you a sneak peek into our digital lives so you can get to know us better and see where we came from and how we've gotten to where we are (and why we're still determined to go further!).

Your digital path may be different from ours, but let us show you how ours unfolded.

AUDREY'S STORY

I treaded into the Internet waters in early 2006 after self-publishing my book, *Preconception Plain & Simple: A Deliciously Smart and Sexy Guide in Preparing for Pregnancy*, with my mother. The book, filled with tidbits to enhance conception, came from my own experience; I wanted to conceive without the stress that seemed to consume so many women around me. From the book, we created a preconception community, PinksandBlues.com, for hopeful moms-to-be. Women came to PinksandBlues to share thoughts and chat. Even after women conceived, they looked to me and our website for motherhood advice. I should've realized then that I was starting a brand. But it's like the nose on your face—it's hard to see when it's right in front of you.

As my family grew bigger (by June 2008, I had four boys, three and a half years old and under), PinksandBlues.com became more of a family product review site. My special area was fashion. I'd learned so much working for Donna Karan, and, even with four boys and the daily threat of spit-up, I accessorized every outfit, wore makeup and cool boots, and read *Vogue* in my "spare" time each week. I still had a great and deep passion for fashion, and my readers felt it and connected with it. Slowly but surely, I began to talk less and less about how to become a mom and more and more about the clothes moms should be wearing. I woke up every morning excited to write. I felt my authentic self emerging.

My mom, sister, and I wisely rebranded the site at this point. Pinksand Blues became MomGenerations.com. We each got a voice; my mother was the voice of the wise grandparent; my sister wrote about being a mom of dogs; and I completely owned the fashion space.

My audience was ready for my full-throttle fashion approach. I began getting daily queries: "How do you tie a scarf?" "Where is the best place to find a little black dress?" "How do you apply mascara without making a mess?" Clearly, I wasn't doing enough for my audience if all these questions weren't being answered.

So on January 1, 2009, with the blessing of my mother, sister, and burgeoning family, I launched 365 Days of Fashion Advice for Moms, a special and very popular offshoot of MomGenerations.com. I loved giving real fashion advice to moms, and, as a real mom, I wanted to be in the mom fashion space because it is my passion.

And it was intense. I needed a new piece of content to post every single day—no questions asked. Fashion is a very visual medium; you need to show women how to do it. I couldn't just write about it and expect big turnouts. So I started developing videos. I put myself in front of the camera three to four times a week. I'd interned at an ABC affiliate in Providence, Rhode Island, during my junior year of college and loved the camera work, even then. I knew I needed to tell a quick story—two minutes max—because moms don't have much longer than that! People took notice immediately. I showed women how to see if pants fit without trying them on (yes, it can be done!) and taught them how to cruise T.J.Maxx for fashion finds. I did mom-makeover segments and fashion "don'ts" segments. Sometimes all four of my boys were (and still are) featured in my videos; if they were underfoot, they made the cut.

To spread the gospel of 365 Days, I created a pretty vast social media footprint, immersing myself in Twitter, Facebook, LinkedIn, and YouTube. Between the videos and social networking, the response was incredible. Traffic doubled, then tripled, then I just stopped measuring.

Finding followers was what I was most "worried" about. I knew I needed other big bloggers (many of them moms) to support me, or I was never going to make it to the level I wanted. But I wasn't sure what to expect when it came to making overtures and introductions. Would it be like high school all over again? The athletes? The "cool" kids? The smart ones? The fashionistas?

Fortunately, when I started blogging, there happened to be a wave of other mothers starting around the same time. Colleen was one of the first people I met online, and I just hit it off with her immediately. We understood each other. We bounced questions off each other. We wanted each other to succeed. For lack of a better word, we were on the same "team." There were about six other Digital Moms with whom I also became close around that time, and we forged amazing business relationships and friendships. One thing that's important to note is that there's room for everyone—every tribe, every group, and every niche—in the digital space. And you can find a way to succeed and find personal satisfaction on your own terms.

That's why I love this world—not every story or every ending is the same. My definition of success is probably even different from Colleen's. The beauty is in really finding a few core people whom you connect with, can grow with, and can learn from. It's like finding that group of best friends at work; it's that essential. As odd as this sounds, because it's so true, I'm better friends with some women online, whom I physically see once or twice a year, than I am with women who live in my own town. You really connect with other women that quickly!

Where's the money, you ask? My first big break moneywise came with an invitation from Lifetime in January 2009. It was the first time a major company/brand/organization took notice of me. They hired me as one of their beauty/style editors on LifetimeMoms.com to provide weekly original content for them. I remember the call. My heart was racing with excitement. They liked what I had to say. They liked the advice I was giving moms. They wanted to pay me to do the work I already loved doing for free.

Then Walmart called. I didn't know it then, but I was being invited to join an elite group of mommy bloggers—the Walmart Moms—to help the store communicate with its mommy shoppers. My goal: to help other moms find fashionable and affordable clothing in the Walmart aisles. I loved knowing that some of my fashion and beauty advice could help moms and families.

After Walmart it seemed as if the floodgates opened. I was invited to walk the red carpet at the People's Choice awards, and the next day I joined Tim Gunn and Gretta Monahan at the Nokia Theatre to talk about the celebrity outfits worn at the People's Choice awards for PeoplesChoice.com; the viewing audience was surely millions of people.

Then, in September 2009, Rachael Ray called. I was invited on air to show Rachael and her viewers how to fashionably accessorize school notebooks (where crafting and fashion meet, you might say). Audience size: many, many millions.

Other invitations promptly followed:

- Interview with the *New York Times* about my role as Land O'Frost Mom Ambassador.

- Getting to walk the runway with Colleen at a Tide-sponsored Geren Ford show at Mercedes-Benz Fashion Week.

- Being chosen to receive six Frigidaire products for my household and vlog about my experience.

- Being asked to pose in a national Estée Lauder Breast Cancer Awareness campaign with my mom and sister. Our generational photograph was then featured in Women's Wear Daily.

- Covering the People's Choice Awards for Tide, Teen Choice Awards Swag Suite for T.J.Maxx/Marshall's, and Emmy Awards for Suave.

- Invitations to speak at numerous social media/blogging/women conferences and panels, including Jeff Pulver's Soc-Comm 2009, Blissdom Conference 2010, Southern New England Women's Conference, and Boston's Publicity Club.

My four sons (William, Alexander, Benjamin, and Henry) are my inspiration. I started this for them because I wanted to be working from home.

But I don't want to pretend it's perfect. It's the middle ground, but that doesn't mean I have the motherhood/work balancing act perfected. My sons don't always understand that I'm on a conference call. They don't understand deadlines. They don't understand to-do lists. I try my best to work around them, but it doesn't always work. This is my life, and there are days I'm online for more than twelve hours. My job is making those twelve-hour days the exception, creating boundaries and schedules that work for me and my family. I try to make most of my conference calls at naptime. If I'm on the phone and the boys are crying or need me, I'm honest with the person on the other end. This is my life. Success for me is and always will be creating a work environment that allows me to be at home with my sons and still contribute financially to the household. To see my sons go off to school, and come back again. It's the little moments throughout the day that warm my heart.

But to be perfectly clear, I spent the first part of my blogging career earning nothing. Not. A. Penny. From 2006 to 2008, I was literally a free agent. My husband took on the role of providing for our family because he believed in what I was trying to build. It's funny, though—once my time and expertise began to be compensated, I knew the compensation needed to keep coming. I set up an LLC and a bank account and loved looking at my business name on the bank statements. I loved being able to contribute to the household coffers again. I didn't and still don't splurge much on myself. But . . . of course, I have my eye on a Louis Vuitton overnight bag. I am a fashionista, after all!

Ever since I was a child, I've believed in happily-ever-afters. When I see my life right now, I feel happiness and contentment and excitement. I love what I do. Not many people can say that. I want to keep pushing myself to create more content. I want to show women that they can attempt to "have it all." It's not easy, but it's all mine. Created and shaped by me. The terms of engagement dictated by me. That is my own version of my own happily-ever-after (and maybe adding a little girl to my brood of boys someday!).

COLLEEN'S STORY

I was busily climbing the corporate ladder with an Ivy League MBA when I got pregnant for the first time in 2005. Hormones, a sense of duty, and the mommy instinct kicked in immediately, and I knew I didn't want to return to a sixty-hour-a-week job after the baby was born.

I told my boss at Sanofi-Aventis Pharmaceuticals that I wanted to take advantage of the company's six-month maternity leave option. At the time, I couldn't tell you what I thought that white lie was buying me other than a sense of job security, but I just knew I needed to put the paid "pause" in place.

Surprisingly, long before the six-month leave was up, something had shifted. I still wanted to be home with my baby girl, but I wanted something else too. I was emotionally maxed out but intellectually unsatisfied. The lonely, isolated lady in me was seeking connection to the world outside the nursery, but to what? My a-ha! moment took shape after I'd made a forty-mile trek to the Coach outlets with my three-month-old daughter Mackenzie (or Kenzie, as I like to call her) to score designer pocketbooks (worth some $4,000) that I would promptly flip on eBay for a sweet profit of about $1,000.

The entrepreneur in me was sprouting wings. I'd found a way to quickly earn some cash from home. My quick calculations and short-term test of selling on eBay showed I could easily earn $1,000 per month. Though I had no desire to be an online sales maven, I cannot tell you how incredibly satisfying that earning power felt. And if you've ever bought or sold on eBay, you know the excitement of an auction is addictive. I began to wonder just what kind of long-term digital career I could have from home—a "job" that didn't involve stocking up on thousands of designer handbags in my guest room, especially when keeping so many of them was so tempting! A job that used my skills as an entrepreneur, marketer, mother, and addict of beautiful products.

I never set out to establish a Classy Mommy brand. Like many great ideas, it all started on a whim. Kenzie had been crying literally all day long. The house was a disaster, as usual. Everything had been "baby baby baby" for the past four months. One eBay auction aside, I felt like my brain was withering into a pile of mush, and I had zero knack for domestic duties. I needed to do something, anything, for a little intellectual stimulation—and I needed to do it every day.

My husband, resident tech geek and web addict, suggested that I start my own blog. It was a passing comment, spoken while heading out the door. But the next day, I took his suggestion to heart. My first blog post was a photo of Mackenzie wearing bunny ears in her ExerSaucer for her first Easter.

I quickly followed up with a post the day after, a product review of $200 wood crayons from Barneys. Just the gift for "Violet" or "Apple," I quipped. I didn't own these crayons, mind you. But my eagle eye (and let's face it, silent longing) for all things high-end baby had led me to them eventually (via countless Google searches for cool products and the guilty pleasure of reading the latest celebrity gossip from *Us Weekly*).

The crayon review lit a flame within me. I loved letting it all hang out. And I began to think I'd enjoy doing more of the same each day. My plan jelled quickly: I'd write about cool mom and/or baby products that I either owned, thought were newsworthy, or coveted when shopping online. My tone would reflect a mix of my economic status (well-off but not filthy rich), my deep-seated frugality, my passion for the latest product trends and styles, and the buyer-beware vigilante in me.

I posted religiously even though I hardly had any readers besides friends, family, and the few moms I'd told about my website. Within a few months of blind productivity, though, something started happening. Other moms— total strangers—were coming to the site to read my advice.

A few months in, I thought it would be fun to add "video reviews" (a.k.a. vlogs) to my offerings. I loved the camera, and when I was young always wanted to be a TV reporter. As a kid, I even auditioned for and was on the game show *Double Dare*.

My first vlog is one of my favorites. I'm feeding organic baby food to nine-month-old Kenzie in a high chair; it's the superexpensive kind the movie stars buy, and I'm trying to show that it's as edible as anything else I've fed the kid over the past several months. Kenzie is performing to specs, oohing and ahhing in all the right places, sated by the very food that Adam Sandler and Michelle Williams feed their kids! Amazing what'll make a mom feel good!

It's important to share that I wrote well over four hundred product reviews and posted them to a database on my website—long before I ever got a free sample from a company. The first was the cutest fleece hat ever, topped with grosgrain ribbon from Lexy Lu Designs, a small mom-owned venture seeking any and all exposure. Then came free shoes from Stride Rite. Then Disney's new DVD releases, products from kid-favorite companies like Little Tykes, and even a Step-2 kitchen. I was stunned. Free stuff.

If I have any regrets from those first start-up months, it was that I didn't reach out to other mommy bloggers sooner. Though I'd lurk on other blogs (thinking: "This is my competition!"), I didn't insert myself into the conversation or try to build friendships and networks. I was so busy growing my own website and my family (which included the addition of my newborn son) that I just didn't have time for more networking online. I was just trying to strike a balance between motherhood and having an outlet for my entrepreneurial fire and product obsession.

But I finally figured out what I'd been missing when I was invited to Johnson & Johnson's Camp Baby Mommy Blogger event in 2008. For the first time I met other moms, face-to-face, who were spending their free time blogging either for fun or as a business, just like me. There were so many women like me. I belonged to something huge. It was the turning point. From there things just cascaded into tons of friendships, collaborations, and future business opportunities.

I learned the value of not only making connections online but following up with in-person meetings when possible. My early conversations online now had faces behind all the handles and avatars. Never discount the importance of meeting someone in real life. That's the trigger for all the real opportunity.

After I met bloggers like me, everything changed. I was two and a half years into Classy Mommy when I received my first invitation to work for a company—Energizer—as a brand advocate for their rechargeables. They wanted to pay me to say nice things about their batteries. It was a big deal, but it wasn't an automatic "yes, of course I will!" I had to decide if I could accept the offer and still be the fast-talking, painfully honest product reviewer who thousands of mommies trusted. In the end, I accepted the gig, as every mom knows just how many batteries all those plastic toys demand if you don't use rechargeables. I couldn't have done it if I didn't believe in the product. But I did, wholeheartedly—and I told my readers so, in case any of them should doubt it. Full disclosure was key. My readers had to know why I was working for/with Energizer, and they had to understand that my unspoken contract with them had not been breached.

After Energizer came an invitation to join the Walmart Moms. After Walmart came TV spots. Then an invitation to work with Audrey for a Healthy Choice campaign. Soon after, Audrey and I were chosen to walk the runway at Fashion Week in New York City for Tide as "real moms." Shortly after, I landed a spokesperson role for Mattel's new line of games for preschoolers and took a Disney Cruise press trip to visit Castaway Cay. Then an invitation to join the Hanes Comfort Crew, which included a trip to Disney World with my family to visit the Parks and Hanes new Design a Tee Store at Downtown Disney. A gig as a superinfluencer for Frigidaire led to a kitchen full of brand-new appliances. Getting hired to be Scrubbing Bubbles spokesperson for the year. Incredible.

The attention put me in the spotlight just when the Federal Trade Commission (FTC) was raising its mighty fist to question the integrity of product review bloggers like me.

Because I'd founded a blog focused solely on product reviews—with a database of some 1,300-plus products by then—ABC News and Fox News were quick to knock on my door for interviews. They asked me the questions I'd asked myself when Energizer first approached—i.e., was it possible to stay honest and work as an advocate for large companies? I told those newscasters what I said above. Full disclosure and a belief in the products I'd been invited to rep were essential. Anything less wouldn't cut it; readers would see right through it, and trust would dissolve. I couldn't risk that, and neither should any blogger doing product reviews.

In reality, the FTC was the least of my problems. I knew I was square with them and my readers. It was my family who was getting the short stick. I repeatedly found myself in bed unable to sleep, thinking about all the vlogging, skyping, and posting I had to do the next day. I was letting business dictate the rules of engagement instead of family. That was backward. I had a newborn, a two-year-old, a business, and no babysitter. I was trying to cram a thirty-hour-a-week job into naptime and evenings. My FedEx woman and UPS man were knocking on my door at all hours with deliveries. I had some 1,000-plus messages in my email inbox, including readers, PR people (offering free tanning solutions, crib mattresses, and juice box flavors, among other products), and the myriad Digital Moms I felt I owed my success to. The professional side of me felt obligations to email everyone a sweet reply with answers signed "xo Colleen." The mom side simply wanted to push a swing or two and not miss the fleeting moments.

It took a near disaster with a TV crew from ABC to actually change my behavior. The scene: my seventeen-month-old clinging to my legs (he was terrified of the camera gear) and my three-year-old whining for more bubbles, Goldfish crackers, and marshmallows while I tried to field questions about working from home. At one point, to get better angles, the TV crew had me turn my back to the kids, which inspired my son to tightrope-walk the top of the couch, at which point the cameraman stopped filming and asked if this was going to work. The short and long answer: no.

I took evasive action. I hired a sitter. I developed a friendship with the delete key on my computer. I turned off Skype for good, as I couldn't afford the extra chatter. The power of being my own boss and being able to make these decisions was incredibly satisfying. I had the option to put my children first, and I chose it.

As for the money, mostly I've socked it away. We call it the "gravy." I never expected to make any, and its existence is still something of a shock. My hope when I began Classy Mommy—and it was a very vague hope—was that if I worked hard on content daily, eventually, someday, something would happen. Something? Maybe I'd earn some revenue. Maybe if I earned some revenue, I'd donate it to charity, a charity like Project Peanut Butter, which helps malnourished children in Africa. Seeing how privileged my new baby was made me want to do more. I'd make the charity my Classy Mommy cause. My husband and I had never planned on my working, since I originally wanted to be a stay-at-home mom. It's wild, but by hanging up the corporate golden handcuffs, I was able to rediscover a whole new me, a whole new digital career. Today, there's enough for charity, impromptu vacations, and home improvement projects we wouldn't have been able to do on one salary. It's thrilling and most unexpected.

After my press last year, I received countless emails from moms across the country asking me how to have a career like mine. I couldn't possibly answer every email, but that collective curiosity—to live out a dream career from home—inspired me to write this book with Audrey.

As you'll read in the chapters to come, we believe there are seven basic steps to finding this middle ground and having a dream career of your own:

1. Find your passion. (Look around; stake out your turf.)

2. Hang a digital "shingle" and start typing.

3. Find your tribe.

4. Make opportunity knock and learn how to answer that door.

5. Manage the Benjamins.

6. Don't forget the children! (Define your version of success and make sure you're truly on middle ground.)

7. Live happily ever after by living your values.

Throughout the book, we'll share our stories—and those of many women who already blog successfully—just to give you a sense of what it's like to become a Digital Mom.

We know this book isn't exactly the latest big-budget thriller. It's more the type of reference book you'll pick up and put down over the course of a week or a month. So some sidebar elements will pop up again and again to make it easy to spot certain kinds of tips and advice as you read:

- **Moms Know Best:** Personal stories and advice from Digital Moms who share their expertise, stories about overcoming obstacles, and tips on what has made them successful.

- **Audrey and Colleen's Tips:** Think of this as "how we did it" or "how we would do it." We'll share our personal experiences and advice and try to break them down into short tips to make it easy for you to breeze through the book and walk away with insider knowledge.

- **Top Five Lists:** Our go-to advice and reasoning in lots of categories, to make it easy to learn the big ideas in a flash as you start your own digital journey.

- Also, we give a **Crash Course in Social Media** on page 207. It's full of helpful terminology and advice that will make the rest of the book easier to understand. You'll be able to familiarize yourself with the varied social media tools available and how best to utilize them.

But first things first. Before we move on to any specifics, let's start at the very beginning—finding the topic that will launch your Digital Mom career. This topic will be the foundation of your entire blogging career, and it will ensure that you are engaged at all times, even when your life becomes complicated (your youngest has been sick and crying all week, the kids' schedules get busy, family and friends are in town, and so on).

So, without further ado . . . **Step 1: Find Your Passion.**

STEP 1

Find Your Passion

The hardest part is always getting started. That very first post. So even if you can't figure out which topic is sure to be your passion, we still encourage you to just get started.

Stacie Haight Connerty, founder of the Divine Miss Mommy, who has more than 49,000 followers on Twitter, shares her best advice for new bloggers. "Just jump right in. Don't wait or put it off because you think you're not ready. Start a blog. Get a free one from WordPress if you need to. Review things around your house if you want to get into reviewing. Write about what you are passionate about. Just start."

Sometimes, just by starting to write you'll find what you do and don't like to write about and where your passions lie. Plus, your writing will improve. We promise. Take a look at our first posts. We cringe a bit when we read them, wishing we had chosen a more riveting topic for our first post, but without that first step we wouldn't be where we are today.

Our First Posts

 AUDREY: MARCH 13, 2007

Looks like I (Audrey) get to be the first one to blog!

Ahhh . . . there's nothing like being eight months pregnant and trying to find the "perfect" outfit to wear to a function.

In my most recent case, last Thursday night at my Nana's eighty-eighth birthday party.

I actually got time that afternoon to shower . . dry and straighten my hair . . . put some makeup on . . . and for all you moms out there who have little ones, we ALL know what a luxury it is to take a shower in peace and not have to worry about rushing rushing rushing—I can thank my husband for taking over the "kid duty"!

When all the finishing touches were done on my hair and face . . . I found myself in my closet trying on about ten pairs of maternity pants, all which fit last week, not fitting this week! I must have put on about fifteen tops . . . some showed too much belly and were really meant for the second trimester! . . . but nonetheless, I kept moving on, knowing the "perfect" outfit had to be among this sea of clothes!

And then my a-ha! moment.

Black leggings . . . a long black sweater dress . . . a striped blouse . . . UGGs . . . I must say, I felt good, and I "thought" I looked pretty damn good—after all, I *am* about thirty pounds heavier than I was at this time last year!

And . . . for the record, I *did* get the husband approval and my two-and-a-half-year-old son even told me I looked "pretty" (which just about smudged my eye makeup as the tears of joy came and "what a big boy he is now" came floating across my mind!).

And so . . . as I made my way around the party . . . laughing and chatting and eating and playing with the kids and having a great time . . . I came across my Nana (the birthday girl!) talking with my father. Now . . . my Nana is *known* for not filtering anything that she says—let me definitely add that in *now*! . . . But, my father looks over at me and says to my Nana, "Can you believe this girl? Look at her belly—it's getting to be that time!"

To which my Nana responded, "Put that belly away. I hate how you girls dress nowadays. You look stupid in all these tight fitted clothes showing off your belly."

OK . . . maybe ten seconds of silence, waiting for the "I'm just kidding . . . you look great . . ."

But nothing.

So I replied, "Well, Nana . . . I like my outfit. This is what feels good and comfortable. And to be honest with you, when you were pregnant, everyone wore clothes that made them look 50 pounds heavier than they really were!"

And she replied back, "Not me . . . I wore nice fitted suits that made me look pregnant. Not sexy!"

I love my Nana! She's a character!

But . . . my point in all of this is . . . WHY DO PEOPLE FEEL THEY CAN COMMENT ON WHAT YOU LOOK LIKE AND WHAT YOU WEAR WHILE YOU'RE PREGNANT!?

I want to wear clothes that make me feel good . . . look good . . . even sexy! I spend time caring about what I look like . . . and like to spend money on things that I know I will get good use out of!

I guess a funny side note would be . . . I loved my outfit so much, I wore it again to two more functions that we had this past weekend!

COLLEEN: MAY 16, 2006

Mackenzie's celebrating her first Easter morning in style. Playing in the Exersaucer and wearing her bunny ears. Gotta love that smile—it is tough to catch on film!

So, just what is your passion? And how do you find it?

pas·sion—noun: any powerful or compelling emotion or feeling

Many people assume that we plunged into our digital careers for the swag, that our passion for freebies fueled our digital work the way nothing else could. Gong. Wrong. No way.

Free Play-Doh. Free shoes from Stride Rite. Free dishwashers. Free family vacations to Disney World. Certainly those are perks of our success (and they weren't lying on our doorsteps when we began, for sure), but this whole ride, from start to finish, has been about succeeding—on our own terms—at careers from the comfort of our own homes, right beside our families.

Before all that swag, before all that branding and networking, Skyping, and vlogging, we asked ourselves one simple question. Everything else followed from there. The question: what is my passion? The answer is what fueled us for the next four years. The answer is what has led to our respective successes. The answer is key.

Now you must find your answer.

PASSION IS NOT A CLICHÉ

All this talk of passion matters—more than you can imagine. The word might sound clichéd, but it's central to being successful in the digital realm. If you don't do something you're passionate about, you'll end up in a boring gray cube (metaphorically speaking . . . or maybe literally, if you're not careful) instead of having a fulfilling cyber-career, no matter what you do. And when we're talking about a digital career on the web, we mean any career centered on the written word, pictures, videos, and a great topic on which you are the expert.

When it comes to the written or spoken word, passion truly does shine through—whether in tone or in the depth of insight shared—and it will differentiate you from everyone else. Ultimately, readers, viewers, and customers will lose interest if you don't have a high level of enthusiasm and exuberance for your business. You simply can't fabricate amazing content and make up stuff day after day.

WRITING ABOUT YOUR PASSION IS NOT WORK

Remember, another critical reason to find your passion is that if you are passionate about something, then it won't feel as much like work and will be far easier to squeeze into your daily routine—even when you are still working full time and juggling the kids. Believe us, with six kids ages six and under between the two of us, it can be done.

The extra hour at night when you could be sleeping is now an hour of extra fun. When the kids sleep in an extra hour, it's exciting to write a blog post or fulfill orders for the handmade blankets you sell on Etsy. On the other hand, if you pursue something you aren't passionate about, you set yourself up for failure; when you are your own boss, it will be exceedingly difficult to pull yourself away from your family or your favorite TV show to work.

Finally, this whole blog thing requires persistence, and persistence, in turn, requires passion. That's the secret at the beginning. For the first days, weeks, and months, you'll feel as if you are talking to yourself. You need to take this time to attract readers, and you'll do this through your love for your topic. Believe us—if you're into fly fishing (and we can guarantee you there are other moms who are into fly fishing), writing about it with zest and life and passion will draw readers to you like flies to ointment (pun intended). At the end of the day, if you aren't talking to yourself about something you love, what's the point? If you don't care—if it's just about the money—chances are no one else will care, either.

WHEN YOU WERE A LITTLE GIRL, WHAT DID YOU WANT TO BE WHEN YOU GREW UP?

You know—that time in your life when it was possible to do anything, be anything, and it was just about *you*? (And we mean that in a good way, not a selfish way.) That's the way it was for a good twenty-something years. Passion was all around you and within you. Passion to run and play. Passion to do well in school. Passion for a particular boy. Passion to make the soccer team. Passion to get the part in the school play. Passion to dress like your older sister. Passion was the one thing you could count on, because it was a feeling you felt from the top of your head to the bottom of your toes. It was a feeling you couldn't put out. It ignited everything in you.

Fast-forward to the present day.

Do you still have passion for what you're doing? Did you love to knit before there was no time in your life for it? Are you passionate about cycling? Collecting vintage dishes and selling them on eBay? Debating current events? Making money, money, and more money?

FINDING THE TIME TO DISCOVER YOUR PASSION

What if you gave yourself the authority to "press pause" and examine yourself top to bottom? It doesn't have to be hard to reflect on your life. You just need to do it! Fifteen minutes a day is more than enough time. It's those small moments of reflection that can ultimately make a big difference.

Everyone's "press pause" moment is different. It may mean taking a week off from work (not everyone has the financial flexibility to do that); it may mean asking your husband to make dinner for two weeks, so you can go for long thoughtful walks from 6 to 7 p.m. (with night reflectors on, please). It may be hopping online for your thirty-minute lunch break at work. However you pull off your pause, and however many favors you now owe as a result, please believe us that this step is absolutely essential.

Sometimes the pause button is pressed for you by circumstance. Think "had to quit job cuz couldn't afford day care" or "got laid off." Seize the moment if those scenarios happen to you, and get busy reflecting on your life and where you want it to go.

A FEW QUESTIONS FOR YOU

We're far from self-help experts, but we've learned a few rules in the process of finding our passions. The first rule is to ask yourself the hardest of all questions: *Am I truly happy with my current career status?* If no, a slew of questions follows:

1. If you're not happy, why do you think that is?

2. Who is doing what you would love to be doing? Can you do this, too?

3. What challenges are holding you back from doing something different?

If you've spent the past several years working for "the man" in between juggling day care drop-offs, ear infections, and car-pools for soccer practice, or the past ten months at home breastfeeding, changing diaper after diaper, wiping up drool, and talking baby talk (bless the moms with multiples!), it's likely that you haven't thought about your true passion in a while. And the beauty of motherhood is that there's nothing wrong with that. But after the fog of early motherhood begins to fade . . . you're left with *you*.

In this chapter we'll help you discover (or rediscover) what gets your emotional motor revving. Why? Because for the first time in a long time, you're not applying for a job or taking somebody else's lead. You're the lady in charge. So why would you pick anything except the best thing you can think of doing—the thing you've always been destined to do?

Now we understand that thinking about passion sounds like a luxury you can hardly afford right now. Between picking up goldfish crumbs, singing nursery rhymes all day, defusing temper tantrums, watching kids' shows, and making your hundredth PBJ of the week, who has time to listen in on her perpetually ignored emotions and desires?

But what if, for once, you put listening to yourself at the top of your list?

Moms Know Best: Passion Stories

HEATHER HERNANDEZ'S PASSION STORY

Heather was a civil engineer before she had kids. Then, when returning to her chosen career proved untenable, she started a blog called Freebies4Mom. The name says it all. She loved the thrill of the freebie and sensed that others would, too. She teaches her blog readers and more than 100,000 Facebook fans how to take advantage of free samples and other promotions by major companies. She says freebies are a great way to try new products at no cost, get free full-size samples, save money with coupons and rebate offers, and most important, spoil yourself. Her blog became so popular that she was able to give up her day job and is now a stay-at-home mom and part-time blogger. She's appeared on *Tyra, Inside Edition,* and more.

My passion for helping others save money motivated me to start blogging in October 2007. My family's need to cut expenses led to my hobby of finding freebies on the web and learning how to save money on everything I bought for my family. When Barilla offered free pasta and sauce for a year (a $70 value), I started to email a few of my friends because I just had to share it! I knew that if the freebies I found were helping my family stay on budget, surely they would help others, too. I get a secret thrill whenever I help someone. I think as mothers we are trained to help others, and many find it intrinsically rewarding the way I do. But my challenge was, how do I help more than just a few of my friends? After receiving a stern warning from Yahoo! that I was sending so many emails that they thought I might be a spammer, I had to take my freebie sharing to a new platform.

My friend suggested starting a blog, and my first response was "I don't know how!" I barely knew what a blog was, let alone how to create one. Well, after a little push from my friend, I discovered Blogger and learned to blog, network, and market myself. I was unexpectedly successful at growing my audience, and before I knew it I was on national TV. Now when I share a freebie, I share it with thousands. Blogging is my new passion, and I get paid to do what I love: helping others save money while filling their mailbox with freebies.

Freebies4Mom
www.freebies4mom.com

SARAH FREYMOYER'S PASSION STORY

Finding herself bored at home, Sarah was always surfing the web to find activities for her three-year-old daughter and one-year-old son in the suburbs of Philadelphia. There wasn't much online for her. She realized she was the most passionate activity researcher out there, and that no one could answer her questions better than she could. With a little work, her Chester County Moms blog was born. Sarah threw herself into finding fun local activities for little kids and helping local moms connect with each other in real life. She provided local content about her own neighborhood and suburban community, and it lit a fire. Today, Sarah works with all the local restaurants, malls, parks, museums, zoos, gyms, music classes, and other organizations to feature special events, calendars, coupons, and so on. Even better, these local businesses are now paying her to consult with them on their social media strategy, and sometimes they even hire her to manage their Facebook pages.

Chester County Moms
www.chestercountymoms.com

ANDREA DECKARD'S PASSION STORY

In the spring of 2007, Andrea was expecting her third child and found out he had a kidney condition that would likely require costly surgery. Months after the diagnosis, she started collecting coupons, shopping online at cash-back sites, even signing up for surveys and focus groups to earn a little money. While she wasn't going back to work, the savings (and some earnings) were sort of like an income for her family. Her son had kidney surgery in October 2007. A year after surgery, she was still going strong and had been able to save $6,500 on grocery spending alone, tracking all her receipts. The Savings Lifestyle was born out of her fierce passion to tell others what she'd learned: "My goal is that the blog will convey hope and encouragement to anyone who stops to read. I strive to tell my story and show each person that regardless of the situation—be it financial, emotional, or health—there really is light at the end of the tunnel." Since its inception, the Savings Lifestyle has grown to receive 250,000 page views a month.

The Savings Lifestyle
www.savingslifestyle.com

You never know—sometimes finding your passion forces you to make life-changing decisions. As many moms know, that's not always easy to do, especially when we have other people depending on us. Changes can't be made overnight; they need time to develop. That's the beauty in defining your passion, though: once you know it and have it, you can put a plan into motion. Small steps forward are always better than standing still.

A NARROW BUT DEEP INTEREST

Odds are that somewhere across the millions of people and eyeballs online, someone else shares your passion, no matter how unique it may seem. The web is powered by highly targeted rich content. The smallest topic in the world might attract many followers and readers. That's why finding a precise passion to be an expert in is so important.

When you're assessing your passions and figuring out what might translate into a career, be sure to consider your level of focus within your passion. For example, say that traveling is your ultimate passion in life. You need to decide if you should just write about traveling in general or cover a narrow niche subset, such as travel and security, budget travel, family travel, or travel in Asia. You get the idea.

Audrey couldn't begin to count how many fashion and style and beauty blogs there were when she began her posts. But in all that fashion din, no one was blogging about fashion, style, and beauty just for moms—and hardly anyone was blogging *daily* about fashion, style, and beauty for moms. It was virtually an undiscovered niche. So even if you have a passion for a broader topic or niche, keep digging deeper. You will find your gem.

Top Five Ways to Find Your Passion if It's Not 100 Percent Obvious to You

1. Ask friends and family what they feel you're an expert in.

2. Visit eBay and Craigslist. Look at all the categories! What topics make you want to click and read more?

3. View your browsing history on your computer. Do you see any common patterns? Odds are that you're consuming content online you truly find interesting.

4. Take five minutes and slowly walk around your house, scanning

each room. What things pull at your heart? Inspire you? Bug you?

5.   Imagine that you've just won a billion dollars. What would you do in your free time?

Moms Know Best: Follow Your Nose for Passion

IN CASE WE HAVEN'T PROVED OUR PASSION CASE YET, HERE'S FURTHER PROOF THAT PASSION RULES.

Rookie Moms: www.rookiemoms.com

Two best friends, Heather Flett and Whitney Moss, were moms at home with their babies when they shared a secret with each other: They were a bit bored. (Gasp, right!?) But they still felt that staying at home with their kids was the right thing to do. Fueled by their passion for motherhood, their friendship, and a desire to electrify their boring days, they started the blog Rookie Moms. Categorized by children's ages, the blog gives activities every day that can be done at home and/or out and about in the "real world." Their ever-popular blog inspired them to write *The Rookie Mom's Handbook*.

Mamavation: www.mamavation.com

Leah Segedie created Mamavation Sisterhood to inspire and teach other Digital Moms about healthy living practices to combat obesity. Leah herself has lost over 170 pounds. Her zest for life, passion, and determination to spread her "mamavation" mission is incredible. She's brought together thousands of women through social media and has created an open and honest destination online where women can go to start changing their lives. Leah's all about helping them take that first step.

Deal Seeking Mom: www.dealseekingmom.com

Tara Kuczykowski is a professional blogger and stay-at-home mother of five. Knowing that raising a large family can be a financial challenge, Tara created a money-saving blog, Deal Seeking Mom. Her passion is to show people in the United States how to stretch their budgets with coupons and still have money left for occasional splurges. Tara has emerged as the go-to money-saving mom online and has helped thousands and thousands of families save money.

Green Your Décor: www.greenyourdecor.com

Jennae Petersen created the uber-amazing Green your Décor blog out of frustration in her attempts to find stylish, sustainable, and eco-friendly decorating products for her home. Her passion is sharing her "green" finds and showing people that you don't have to sacrifice the planet to look good. She is *the* green-decorating destination online for moms.

Traveling Mom: www.travelingmom.com

Kim Orlando started Traveling Mom as a way to connect moms who travel. She shares tips, products, and fabulous travel destinations and has created travel communities online. She shares everything that a mom needs to know about traveling and now has a staff of writers who contribute content on even more important topics, including special needs travel, traveling with teens, and grandparenting travel. You name it—she covers it.

PASSION + SKILLS

As we said earlier, passion drives the bus, but you'll need to pair that passion with skills like networking, talking a blue streak, writing thousands of words in less than an hour, improvising in front of a camera, and so on. You need to think about what skills from your current or former careers might translate into a digital career, and pair those with your passion.

Now's the time to grab a pencil and a blank sheet of paper, draw a line down the middle, title the left column "Skills" and the right column "Would Rather Not," and get honest about the sorts of work you should be doing online and the work you should not. Some words that might appear on either side of those columns: budgeting, talking, writing, managing money, bossing people around, listening, baking, selling, designing, brainstorming, teaching . . . you get the idea.

MOMS WHO USED THEIR PROFESSIONAL SKILLS TO LAUNCH THEIR DIGITAL CAREERS

Whitney Wingerd, founder of Mommies with Style, came from a new media background prior to becoming a mother. Writing, editing, and managing a new media publishing house and software company prepared her well for a solo business that leaned heavily on social media. According to Whitney, "Motherhood [and a dysfunctional need to shop for nice things on a regular basis] was the final piece of the puzzle that became my blog and business." Her blog covers what real moms are using and buying for their kids or themselves. She's built a community of writers and message boards where moms can chat about their finds—what works and what doesn't.

Before having kids, Caroline Ritter worked in New York City as a Jill-of-all-trades in the fashion industry, landing a stint at Ralph Rucci, a management position in Nordstrom's couture collections, and a job designing stores for Lilly Pulitzer. Then the babies came, and fashion took a backseat—until Caroline pressed pause and looked around. "I needed a creative outlet. I started making burp cloths for my son, Miles, because I didn't like the ones I could find in stores. Then I thought, *Other people would like these,* and decided to create my own line called 'Lina Bean' and sell my products online.

For as long as I can remember, I've wanted to have my own business. I always thought it would be a boutique, and maybe someday it will; but right now Lina Bean lets me make my own hours and create new things all the time, which is perfect."

Do you see what we mean? The possibilities are absolutely endless! There's so much room out there to go and create; it's just a matter of getting out there and doing it. A mom could bring her former journalist skills to YouTube, her PR background to start her own PR company from home, or her master of fine arts and her sewing skills to become an eBay textile mompreneur.

Moms Know Best: Sometimes Your Passion Is Simply Motherhood

"Is it okay that my true drive, true passion is wanting to stay home with my children?" Heather Allard asked herself as she considered her options within the digital space. "That was the motivation behind the businesses I've started"—Swaddleaze and TheMogulMom.com—"wanting to stay home with my kids, see all their 'firsts,' and earn an income from home."

It's completely normal to be passionate about motherhood. But if motherhood is the only item on your passion list, that doesn't mean you put this book down and throw in the towel. Motherhood is a subject that hundreds of Digital Moms have mined for business ends. And if that's the canvas on which you too will paint, great. Join us! But consider asking yourself a few specific questions before you jump into this digital realm.

For starters, what's your specific passion within the motherhood category? Is it cooking for your children?

Is it coming up with activities and outings for you to do together? Did it take you a long time to become a mother, and you want to talk about it with other moms? Do you love dressing your kids? Do you love finding hidden gems—including places to go, toys to buy, books to pick up—that you're excited to share? Are you passionate about organic foods and an eco-friendly lifestyle for your family? It's important to carve out a niche before you dive in.

Also, ask yourself how much you want to share about your family before you commit to this direction. You'll be connecting with thousands and thousands of other mothers and possibly non-moms. How much of your personal life, your words, your family photos do you want out there?

This question isn't meant to stop you in your tracks. Really, it's a question for anyone who's hung a shingle online, anyone who's talking and sharing her personal stories. You must ask yourself in advance: what and how much should I share? And where do I draw the line for privacy's sake?

YOUR BLOG IS YOUR SOAPBOX

As a blogger you can use your posts to discuss, share, and promote any content you wish. Catherine Connors's blog, HerBadMother.com, focuses on parenting, but she's also been able to share the story of her nephew Tanner. Tanner suffers from Duchenne's muscular dystrophy, a disease that won't be cured in his lifetime and will eventually take his life.

Catherine does something on her blog that is remarkable: she brings us into Tanner's life in such a powerful, important, and necessary way. She's helping him chase his dreams—beautiful dreams that he wants to feel and touch and do in his lifetime—and through her blog, she's making them happen. What's most extraordinary about Catherine, though, is not that she's been able to educate the world about DMD but that she's been able to bring a face to it. She has made Tanner known to thousands of people who are praying for him, rooting for him, and doing what they can to bring his dreams to fruition.

CREATING SOCIAL CHANGE

Bloggers create platforms for their content, and it's always inspiring to find bloggers who decide to use that platform to create social change. These moms demonstrate a strong conviction for their causes, and they truly take their personal passions and make them known, visible, and exposed for the world to see. For them, posting a blog is just another way to make a difference.

For instance, MOMocrats.com is a site where mothers from across the United States come together to write about politics from a parent's perspective. The site was founded by Stefania Pomponi Butler, Beth Blecherman, Glennia Campbell, and a few other moms because they wanted to establish a place online where progressive Democratic women could learn from one another and express their views. They've had guest posts from Michelle Obama, and Barack Obama answered their questions directly during the Democratic primary.

SOME FINAL TAKEAWAYS

As a refresher, here are the two major points we've hit in this chapter:

First, so many inspiring and incredible mompreneurs online are changing the world through their words, making money, and truly defining a new way to work from home. They each began their digital lives with passion for a subject, and this passion anchored them. As a result, it didn't matter if no one was listening to their tweets, posts, or vlogs at the beginning. They still loved what they were doing. Second, persistence matters. And you can persist only if you're passionate about what you're doing.

As we wrap up this chapter on finding your inner drives and passions, we want to give you a closing prod—so that there's no way (nope, none) you leave this chapter without the proper dosage of inspiration and direction. Below, find a list of some fabulous online profiles you might consider trying on for size to see if the shoe fits.

DOES THIS SOUND LIKE YOUR DIGITAL PROFILE?

Fabulous gourmet blogger
Martha Stewart in miniature
Coupon-hungry mom
Trendsetting fashionista
Fitness guru
Organic foodie
"Greener" mommy
Tech geekette
Queen of entertaining
Flailing but happy entrepreneur
Shopping machine
Town hall journalist
eBay addict
Facebooking scrapbooker
Family photo obsessive
Real Simple organizing expert
Devoted single mom
Divorcée paving the way
HGTV-caliber interior designer
Bookworm

Clearly, we feel responsible for revving up your emotional motors. Your digital future could be based on a hobby, an obscure interest, a life stage you're fixated on, or simply a business skill you'd love to put to good use in some capacity or other while being at home with your kids. Don't leave this chapter until you're truly ready, because the next step is a big one: **Step 2: Hang a Digital "Shingle" and Start Typing!**

STEP 2

Hang a Digital "Shingle" and Start Typing!

At the beginning, you're just putting in lots of hard work and waiting. Lots of waiting. Posting daily and hoping someone will someday read your posts and that something big will happen. Like going to the gym day after day trying to get in better shape.

—Vera Sweeney, ImNotObsessed.com

Starting a business used to be a high-risk investment. Hefty start-up costs, overhead, employees to pay and insure, and so on. Ugh. Who needs it? With the Internet, start-up costs are typically zero, nothing, nada. It's one of those "too good to be true" truisms that actually is true. The only risks to you are emotional and physical, for the most part—such as sleeplessness as you toss and turn on a great idea that you can't wait to post to your site, obsessive-compulsive smartphone checking, and occasional blows to your confidence when no one shows up to your posting, just to name a few.

Now that you've found your passion, you have no excuse but to jump online and do something about it.

HANG THAT SHINGLE

When a person decides to work for herself rather than for "the man" and declares her intention publicly, we call it hanging a shingle. On that shingle is your name or the name of your business, so make it catchy (for some tips, see "Moms Know Best" below). Hanging it requires chutzpah, but more than that it requires a plan, time, and a willingness to work for little returns (at least at first)—all for the sake of running one's own show. Some Digital Moms hang a digital shingle when they're still occupied with their full-time jobs or full-time motherhood, and the shingle is simply a declaration of things to come. That's fine. Whether you're declaring the beginning of your new digital venture or actually digging in and posting regularly, hanging that shingle is a big and essential first step. It says, "I'm here. And I've got something to say."

Five Tips to Creating the Perfect Site Name

1. Use words that cause alarm bells to go off in your head and everyone else's—words like savings, mom, crafts, coupons, deals, style, gourmet.

2. Make the name short, sweet, and easy to spell! Avoid wordplay that can be confusing or hard for people to remember.

3. Make sure the name you choose is not already trademarked by another company or organization or is already in use. You can learn more about trademarks at www.uspto.gov/.

4. Own the URL (uniform resource locator) for your site. Visit Go Daddy, One and One, Domain Discover, or another web host-

ing company for how to buy. It will help you avoid trademark issues down the line, when and if you hit it big. It's inexpensive, too—about $10 per year on average. If your first-choice name is not available as a .com, you should think of another name. Opting for .net or .tv just won't be as accessible for your readers. After buying your domain name, make sure you then buy the .tv, .net, and .org names as well so you own the entire spectrum. If possible, you should buy the domain name for your own personal name, too, if it is available (e.g., www.janedoe.com).

5. Choose a name you can grow with. If your blog mentions pregnancy, keep in mind that you're pregnant for only forty weeks.

THE VERY FIRST WORDS

Truly, the hardest part of becoming a successful Digital Mom is finding and maintaining confidence. It's likely that not many people will see your very first posts, but what happens when they do? Will they laugh? Will they shout something rude or offensive? Or will they watch quietly while you say or shout what you came to say or shout?

Trust us when we say that we and every popular Digital Mom we know second-guessed herself on the way to that first post. Some of the undermining thoughts that might stand in your way:

1. Who wants to hear what I have to say?

2. How's anyone besides my mom and sister-in-law gonna find me in this "world wide" phonebook?

3. Does anything I say really matter?

4. I can barely handle email. How will I manage an entire website, upload pictures, and potentially post audio and video clips?

5. I'm afraid the computer will crash when I push any unfamiliar button.

6. I'll never learn all the lingo (podcast, vlog, Twitter, Skype, and so on). It all sounds so sci-fi—and I never read sci-fi!

7. I'm afraid that weirdos may reply to my posts. Do I have to respond?

8. I don't want to edit everything I say because I'm afraid my in-laws or my mother will read it.

9. Are there really other moms out there who will relate with me?

10. Will my kids or husband read my stuff and be embarrassed?

TAKE BABY STEPS

Let's pretend, for example, that your passion is collecting and selling vintage dolls. You have a garage full of them, inherited from your family, plucked up at garage sales, and so on. You're ready to buy more and better dolls, and you're ready to unload some of the dolls you've got. Maybe you also want to sell those doll clothes you've been sewing at home. You're considering starting your own blog or website or hitching your wagon to a middleman website such as Etsy (for cottage crafters and their ilk) or eBay (headquarters for auction-based retailers).

Whichever way you go—and there are far more options than just those—you must first find a name for yourself, one that allows other doll obssessers to find you. *Doll Mom? Doll-finder Mommy? Mom's Dolls.* We're not feeling inspired. Take a walk outside or wander around your house trying on names. Wash some more dishes and say some possible names out loud, over the sound of the running water. Keep a piece of scratch paper in your hip pocket for moments of inspiration, or just scribble a few into your ongoing shopping list. Make sure your name both sounds and reads well—that people will understand it when they hear it casually from friends.

Let's say you eventually settle on *Dollmama.* (We must say we like this name, too.) And let's say that for your very first post, you'd like to compare the way you care for your dolls with the way your six-year-old daughter, Sheila, cares for hers (by cutting off their hair and drawing on their skirts). You consider yourself a funny person, and you intend to make people laugh with this and future posts. You also intend to feature one of your gorgeous porcelain dolls in the post because you plan to lure folks in with great story-telling and then hook them with great dolls.

Okay, see, we're getting somewhere. Now, next big decision: do you want *Dollmama* to speak through the written word, through audio, or through video? Those are the "big three" media on the Internet. Almost everyone starts with writing, because it's most familiar. And it's so easy. If you can write an email and attach a picture, you've already got it down!

And once you get the text part down, you can reach for the next media: sound and video. If you know how to talk on the phone and enunciate clearly, you can record audio for your post. You can even create a podcast, which is basically an online radio show. And if you own a Flip camera or similar digital device or know how to operate the camera built into your computer, then you're ready and equipped to shoot a video post today, too. So which is it? Feeling pretty and sassy and love to ham it up? Run for your digital camera. If you feel that your prose and pictures of your dolls should be the main attraction, and you'd rather focus on what you do well, that's fine, too. You can always add on video and audio later if you change your mind.

WHERE WILL MY VOICE/FACE LIVE ON THE WEB? HOW WILL I GET IT THERE?

Once you've decided your medium—whether text, audio, or video—there are myriad locations on the web where you can build your site, or hitch your wagon to an existing site, and begin. And there are just as many tools to choose from to make it all happen. We could fill the rest of this book with advice about how to build a site from the bottom up; which blog platform is best if you decide you don't need to invent the blog from scratch (WordPress, Blogger, Typepad); which retail hub to launch yourself from (Etsy or eBay, for starters); whether to shoot video with a digital camera or a camera built into your computer (a webcam); whether to sell your goods through your own site or through a third party; whether to use iMovie, Windows Movie Maker, Final Cut Pro, or OneTrueMedia to edit movies; and whether to upload to YouTube, Vimeo, OneTrueMedia, Blip.TV, or any other community video-sharing site. In truth, those decisions require you to explore and experiment.

As you can tell, you have a lot of options for all these elements. We'll mention these tools throughout the book. You should visit them all to get a sense of how they work, and then decide which ones support your particular talents and goals, and go from there. However, we also understand that this range of options is pretty intimidating, so below we're going to help you out by sharing our five favorite ways for entering the digital world.

THE FIVE EASIEST WAYS TO LAUNCH YOURSELF INTO THE DIGITAL REALM

It used to be that the only way to quickly launch yourself on the Internet was to create a website or a blog. Those are still great ways, but now we have so many other options. Here's a list of our favorites. If any of the social media terms are unfamiliar or intimidating, or even if you'd just like a refresher, please check out "Crash Course in Social Media" in Appendix A, page 207. It's full of helpful terminology and advice that will make the rest of the book easier to understand!

- **Start with a blog:** We promise that if you go to one of the free blog headquarters on the web (WordPress, Blogger, and Typepad), in less than five minutes you can have your own blog. Seriously, put down this book. Go to your computer and visit Blogger.com (a very easy free blog source for beginners, and where we both started!). Click "Start a Blog" now.

Follow the prompts. You're done. It should take about five minutes. Really. And if you desperately want to read more about blogging (instead of finding out for yourself by just diving in headfirst), consider reading *Blogging for Dummies* and/or *ProBlogger*, or head on over to Desperately Seeking WordPress, a blog about how to blog. And beware—just because blogging starts with you typing doesn't mean it can't end with you behind the camera. Most of the bloggers we know are podcasting and vlogging from their blogs. It's now a three-dimensional blog world.

- **Start with Facebook:** We know you've heard of it, but have you actually signed up? The world changes once you do. First, you'll "friend" family, neighbors, classmates, and even college sweethearts; then your network will suddenly expand as friends of friends find you. The key here is to keep posting your personal or business updates. They don't always need to relate to the business you're trying to start, but it's wise to have consistent content on Facebook. That way followers always know, "Oh, that Digital Mom always has an interesting something or other to share. I'm clicking on over . . . "

- **Start with Twitter:** We know you've heard of this site, too, but you've got to really understand it. In 140 characters or less, people are communicating, forging alliances, partying, fighting international dictators, and on and on. It's instantly gratifying, and it's amazingly easy to find like-minded souls here. It's such a wonderful way to keep yourself connected online with so many different people. It's also very easy, which is helpful and exciting for many women who are looking to jump into the world of social media. How do you get started? Head over to Twitter.com and create a profile and a Twitter handle. We're @AudreyMcClellan (that's right: no D) and @ClassyMommy. Your Twitter handle can be only sixteen characters long. Take it from us—choose a name that is easy to remember and (if you can get it in there) use the word "mom," as this will be an instant way to make friends within the mom community.

- **Start with YouTube:** Here's the place where everyone has a chance to be their own TV star and to broadcast their own stories to the world. Did you know YouTube has over a billion views per day? Certain users stand out and are promoted as they gain popularity. We'll share tips and tricks to making the most of YouTube so your videos get more hits.

- **Start with BlogTalkRadio and podcasting:** Podcasting enables anyone to be an instant reporter and radio host, which can be a huge asset to bloggers or a stand-alone career in itself. Knowing how to create podcasts is incredibly useful, since it gives you a chance to record live phone interviews with celebrities, experts, doctors, professionals, and other guests and to share information with your audience at the time you're gathering it. BlogTalkRadio is our top resource to recommend if you want to start with podcasting. It's free and simple, and you'll be able to record phone conversations over your special dial-in radio show number. Your audience can listen to segments live and even participate by calling in. Even cooler, these segments are preserved forever, and you can embed the audio clip in your own website or blog.

Tools of the Trade

	Reach	Flexibility	Popularity	Ease of Use
Blog	◑	●	◕	◑
Facebook	●	○	●	●
Twitter	◑	○	◕	◔
YouTube	◑	○	●	◕
Skype	◕	○	◕	◑

Moms Know Best: Colleen Starts a Blog (Without Blowing Up the Computer)

Four years ago I thought that creating my own blog was far beyond my technological capabilities, and just getting started was the giant hurdle for me. I couldn't imagine I'd be able to figure it out, as I had no tech experience whatsoever. Somehow I'd screw it up and end up posting in Greek, and no one would read my precious ideas about precious baby products. My husband, a tech geek, disagreed. But he refused to create a blog for me. He said, "If you can write an email and know how to send an attachment or photo, you can blog." I lacked the confidence required, I replied. He disagreed again. And to prove that I was up for it, he did not lift one finger to get me started. "Catch a man a fish, feed him for a day . . . teach a man to fish . . . " Blah blah blah.

I wanted to throw in the towel when I heard that. We were at a stalemate. I might've known how to drill through a database back when I was a professional gal, crunching numbers for a marketing and sales team, but this felt altogether different. Databases existed, and I merely dug through them. My blog did not yet exist. I would have to build its walls, its foundation. I would have to give it a reason to exist, and then I would have to turn the lights on every morning and pretend I knew how to run it. The blog adventure had "failure" written all over it. And my husband's chuckling didn't help matters (his running joke until then was "Every time you walk into my office my computer crashes.").

But one day, when baby Kenzie was happily distracted in her Exersaucer and I was unhappily stewing about my lack of a life outside of domesticity, I bucked up, turned on my computer, and clicked on over to Blogger.com. Ten easy prompts and five minutes later my blog, ClassyMommy. blogspot.com, was born. Amazing. Truly, I found my first blog post to be as easy as writing an email. And also a bit embarrassing—I mean, all that anxiety for no reason at all! I've filled out more confusing DMV forms! And the beauty of leaping through that very small (but seemingly huge) hurdle? I now feel confident jumping much bigger and more intimidating techie hurdles all by myself.

In case Colleen's start-up story didn't make it clear, we are not tech-savvy moms. Colleen was lucky enough to have a husband help her through the technology thicket once she'd begun her Classy Mommy adventure. And Audrey simply hired help. We will share basic tech tips as we progress through this book, but if you want to better understand the moving parts behind blogs and vlogs and podcasts and Twitter and Facebook, and on and on, then you might consider consulting a few books and/or websites that have mastered the art of translating tech jargon into lay-speak. We include a list of good resources in the "Crash Course in Social Media" we mentioned earlier, to help you get started.

SETTING UP YOUR RULES

If you're the sole voice and employee of this new venture, then you'd better get ready to boss yourself around. In other words, set up some rules for yourself, and stick to them. Inconsistency is a deal-killer on the web. Your readers want to return to your site day after day after day, to find the same great advice, reviews, recipes, or products that you offered them the day before. You'll undermine all your start-up efforts if you fail to deliver on the great promise of your initial posts. (Imagine if, one day, you drove up to your favorite local ice cream store, salivating for a Rocky Road scoop, and found the door locked with a sign hanging over the window that said, "We've decided to close from 1 to 4 p.m. today." And then the next day, you went at 4 p.m., and the door was locked again. This time the sign said, "Closed until 4:45 p.m." And then the next day it wasn't open at all, and there was no sign to explain. Pretty soon, you'd just go find yourself another ice cream store with regular and predictable hours.

Here are a few rules we set up for ourselves. They worked, and we recommend them to all rookie Digital Moms:

1. Have a routine. Post every week or every day (most who succeed post at least once a day). Make sure your posts are consistently strong and offer your readers what you've promised to offer (by that we mean that if you promised to talk about your family and your dolls, then don't waste a week of posts talking about liver and onions).

2. Keep an editorial calendar. You can share it with your readers or keep it to yourself, but either way a calendar tells you what you plan to talk about in upcoming days and weeks. It ensures that you're not being repetitive or missing a topic, and it sets up proper expectations.

3. Always talk about something that matters to you; be authentic and real. If everyone on the web is talking about hair implants and you decide to talk about them too, but have no real interest in hair implants, your readers will smell a poser and take off faster than the Road Runner when chased by Wile E. Coyote.

4. After posting, maybe at the end of the day, read any comments and reply to those readers who seem genuinely interested. Replying to comments is the beginning of a process we call finding your tribe (and we devote the whole next chapter to that subject).

5. When possible, title posts as if they're news headlines. Think of something attention grabbing or catchy, such as "One Million Car Seats Recalled." Who wants to read something with a boring title? Don't lose a potential reader at "Hello" if you can help it.

Moms Know Best: Content Is King

Lori Falcon, founder of ACowboysWife.com, MyWooden-Spoon.com, and eLivingMedia.com, is not only a full-time blogger but also a rattlesnake wrangler, mother of three boys, and wife of a real cowboy. She's a self-made blogger who was determined to make something of herself—and she has. She's been blogging for nearly four years and has a reputation for having a never-ending arsenal of amazing content. From the mouthwatering recipes on MyWoodenSpoon.com to breathtaking photos of her men and boys on the ranch, she has us coming back for more every day.

Q: What advice do you have for new bloggers on creating engaging and interesting content?

A: Just be yourself. Be a leader, not a follower. It's okay to follow a few trends, but think outside the box and create your own ideas. Only you will know what's best for you and your audience.

Q: How do you create such refreshing content?

A: When I surf the web, read a magazine, or watch TV, I always find something I can relate to. I take those ideas and jot them down in an editorial calendar. I may not use all the ideas, but they are there when I need them. Just living life makes for some refreshing content, in my opinion.

Q: How do you incorporate your family into your blog?

A: Photos, photos, photos. If I cook my grandma's banana pudding, I take a photo of my son eating it. When my husband builds a pair of spurs, I show them off. I can literally create a post, show nothing but photos of the family or their creations and activities, and get more comments than on a text post. Photos bring out emotion—diverse emotions at that.

LOOKS MATTER, MANNERS MATTER, TIME MATTERS

After you've gotten nice and cozy posting smart blogs or smashing vlogs once a day or once a week—after you've got your groove on and have committed to this venture with all your heart and soul—it's time to think about some polish. Polish is your first confidence boost after that initial burst of energy that got you posting in the first place. Sometimes polish requires a bit of investment (paying for a website designer to create a logo for you, for instance), and sometimes it requires a tube of lipstick, which we hope you already own. Here are a few basic polish pointers we can pass on:

1. **Get yourself a great logo and blog template:** Those are what readers will see every time they come to the front page of your site. They are, for all intents and purposes, your first step toward becoming a brand. Yes, by starting this venture, you're becoming a brand, just like Kellogg's Corn Flakes or DKNY. From this point forward, everything you say and how you look are part of your brand identity. So don't dress your site in pink paisley if the brand identity you seek is modern and sleek.

2. **Make your blog visually interesting:** You know the saying "A picture is worth a thousand words." It couldn't be more true in the online world. Imagine reading a magazine with no photos. Boring, right? So include photos along with your content whenever possible. Sometimes a photo will be all you need for the post. Quite a time saver, too! Down the road you might want to think about investing in a better camera and taking a photography class, doing an online tutorial, or reading a book on digital photography. For now, here are a few pointers:

   • When you upload photos to your blog, choose to display them as large pictures, not tiny ones.

   • Nothing beats natural light. Take photos in daylight when possible.

- Zoom. Zoom closer. Close-ups look fabulous and show so much more detail and individual character than long-shot photos of either objects or people.

- Play with Photoshop or the settings on your camera to edit your pictures. Cropping, getting rid of red-eye, and more can all often be done directly from the camera. Your computer may already have a photo-editing program—check it out. Editing your photos instead of displaying them straight from the camera will do wonders for your images.

- Practice shooting food to make it look good. Good food photography is surprisingly challenging. If you are posting a recipe or sharing details on dining at your favorite restaurant, it's better to have no photo at all than to share a picture that looks unappetizing.

- Think about the composition of your photos before you hit click. Is there a distracting object in the background? If so, change your angle or viewpoint, move the object if possible, or ask your subject to stand somewhere without distraction.

- The "rule of thirds" is a classic photography guideline. Imagine breaking your screen into a three-by-three grid. In a nutshell, this principle suggests that you place the focus of your photo in either the left or the right third of the photo for best results, so the viewer's eye can be drawn to the focus first and then gradually gaze at the rest of the photo. Centering your focal point can actually result in awkward photos rather than the striking shots you can create by using the rule of thirds.

- Practice makes perfect. Take pictures every day—you'll have more material to blog with, and you'll definitely get better at it.

- Check out the blog Digital Photography School for all kinds of tips: www.digital-photography-school.com/

3. **Remember that appearance matters:** If you're going in front of the camera, wear lipstick and a shirt without throw-up or spaghetti sauce on it. The lipstick will give you confidence. The clean shirt will make you feel like a professional. You never know when your video is going to go viral and get a million hits on YouTube.

4. **Skip the music:** This is probably the most subjective advice you'll hear us give. But we stand by it. You may think the music is polish, but it's not. First off, you can't buy the rights to that fantastic music you'd love to feature. And the crummy stuff that's free isn't worth listening to. Finally, music tends to distract visitors from the real feature on your site: your words, audio, or video.

5. **Be yourself and be genuine:** Don't rehearse. Go with the flow and do what feels natural. This method has worked best for both of us. For example, we always do one take when filming vlogs, no matter the outcome. Our videos often include tantruming, wall climbing, or squabbling kids being bribed with marshmallows to quiet down for one-minute-and-thirty-second videos. We never edit out this background chaos. It's become our signature "what's real," and it sets us apart. It is obvious to our readers that we're real moms sharing real advice.

6. **Keep it short and sweet:** If it's a text entry, a podcast, or a vlog, keep it short. We don't even want to watch our own videos after one minute has gone by, so most likely our audience won't want to, either.

7. **Ask compelling, open-ended questions:** If you're going to interview someone, have questions ready, or an entire script. Make sure the questions aren't yes-or-no questions but require the interviewee to answer in depth.

TECHNICAL ASSISTANCE

Several of the steps above require assistance unless you are moderately tech savvy. As we've confessed previously, we are not. Our strengths, instead, lie in our business acumen, our persistence, our desire to keep up with the latest trends, and our comfort in front of cameras. Really, we're still pretty terrified about making changes to our blog templates.

If you hire out for help, depending on the complexity of your blog, you could hire a blog designer for as low as $100 to $500, total. We started a joint blog venture this year with two other friends and paid $500 for the setup of a brand-new site. Pretty inexpensive when you consider that's the only investment we needed to make—besides our own blood, sweat, and tears, that is.

Where can you find a designer? The best way, we think, is to make a list of sites you admire, then email the founders of those sites to find out who designed them. Through this process, you will discover that many mom bloggers moonlight as designers. Melissa Angert at GirlyMama.com is one of them. "My basic blog design is $150, but I offer a 'beginner blog package' as well. This is where I help my client set up the infrastructure that really takes time to build: an 'about me' page, widgets in their sidebars, domain mapping so they can look professional and put together right out of the gate!"

That infrastructure is crucial. If your links don't work and no one can find your post from last week or yesterday, then your business isn't gonna float for very long. If you find prices too high among experienced designers, try posting on Craigslist; specify how much you can afford and make sure that any candidate sends you links to work he or she has done before, so you can see if the sites actually work and look good. On Craigslist you'll very likely find a hungry and talented college kid looking for experience that will cost next to nothing.

Moms Know Best: Tale of Two Vloggers

Esther Crawford, the editor behind ShePosts.com, a news site that reports on the mom social media digital space, knows how to make a "sticky" video. She can claim over 11,000 subscribers on YouTube for her personal channel. In 2007 she was chosen as an official video blogger for the YouTube community and attended the CNN/YouTube presidential debates, which led to a series of political commentary pieces on Fox News; AdWeek, CNET, and AOL. Kmart was so impressed that it brought her on as a social media consultant. She knew she was a success when she got to hug Anderson Cooper.

Q: **What advice and tips do you have for someone who is new to vlogging?**

A:　My best advice is to tell stories. Real stories. Heartfelt, funny, sad, and deeply true stories. It's great if you have a fancy camera, can edit well, have perfect lighting, and all of that. But if you're talking about things that aren't universally interesting, you'll find that a very small audience is interested. However, if you're sharing your take on what's in the news or letting people in to regularly experience life with you, that will grab folks and keep them coming back for more.

Q: **Which of your vlogs or videos have been the most successful? Why do you think it was a hit?**

A:　My most-watched videos were all created on a webcam using basic editing techniques in iMovie. I didn't even know how to really edit until I'd been uploading vlogs for well over a year. My most-watched video of all time has 1.6 million views and is the video where I hit my final weight loss goal. It's been a big hit for a lot of reasons: the timing was right; it's a feel-good story that recaps my journey with striking before-and-after photos; and I'm genuinely excited in it. Plus, I named and tagged the video properly so people searching for before-and-after success stories would find it.

Q: How could you replicate this huge success?

A: The success of some videos, like the one I just described, is not something I can replicate on any given day. However, there are certainly several things that improve the odds of a video becoming a big hit: a hot topic; polarizing opinion; someone famous or infamous; collaboration with other vloggers or bloggers; something genuinely funny; unique footage, perhaps of an event; a captivating thumbnail image; a catchy title; lots of search-friendly keywords so others looking for a video about a specific topic will find your video if it is relevant; anything to do with Lady Gaga—since she's had over a billion views to her videos on YouTube.

Danielle Smith, founder and primary author of Extraordinary Mommy, left mainstream TV news to launch a site focused on the charitable acts of, well, extraordinary mommies. She's scored reporting gigs for Procter & Gamble and Con Agra Foods. She knew she was a success when she was standing on the set of *Desperate Housewives* for her child hunger campaign.

Q: As a former professional TV journalist, what advice do you have for new people starting out doing videos or vlogging?

A: I'm confident that you'll initially find it painful to watch yourself on camera, but truly, the only way to improve—the only way to find that comfort level—is to do it again and again and to watch for mannerisms, tone, and speech patterns that you might want to adjust.

Q: What outside factors influence the quality of a vlog? What should people look out for and try to do?

A: Like it or not, the technical aspects of a vlog definitely influence not only the quality but whether or not people will watch. If they can't see you (you're in front of a window or in a dark room), they can't hear you (you're whispering so as not to disturb people around you, or you're drowned out by background noise), or the camera is shaking like crazy, they will, I promise, turn it off. For the best light, shoot during the day—outside if possible, or facing a window. If you can use a microphone, I recommend it, especially if there is noise around you. Always have your batteries charged and enough room on your disk—there are few things more disappointing than realizing you weren't prepared.

Q: What fashion advice do you have for people going on camera?

A: When you're deciding what to wear, fashionable is great—but distracting is not. Large scarves, heavy jewelry, big hats, crazy logos—they all distract from you and what you're saying. You want people to hear you. Let them embrace all you have to share without confusing them with your attire.

SETBACKS

It may be easy to get yourself started, but the road to success is paved with bumps, detours, sinking feelings, and, well, people flipping you the proverbial bird. We can't lie. It's not fun to receive a rude comment about a post. It's also not fun to prepare what you think is the best post ever and then have almost no one show up to read or listen to it. All those things have happened to all of us. Believe it! Jill Smokler keeps more than

50,000 readers entertained daily at her Scary Mommy Twitter feed, but that doesn't prevent her from getting flames (rude comments) from time to time. She may rank No. 5 on Babble's list of "Top 50 Twitter Moms" and No. 3 on its "Funniest Twitter Moms" ranking. She may be quoted in the *New York Times*, CNN, *Redbook*, and *Ms. Magazine*, but she still remembers when she got her first really mean comment. "Instead of feeling hurt or offended, I was psyched! Finally, someone other than my friends and my mother was reading me! I'd gotten under someone's skin—score! Some of them get to me more than others, especially when they're on issues I am sensitive about, but it comes with the territory. And it beats having only my mom read me."

In short, sharing your opinion or even your wares (if you're a retailer) will always expose you to criticism. In the digital space, as in real life, not everyone you meet is going to agree with you or like what you're offering. Expect to get hot responses to hot topics (e.g., politics, religion, home-schooling, breastfeeding, green living, Walmart). As for responding to negative comments that are extremely nasty—written by what people call a troll in the Internet space—our advice and personal strategy is to not reply to these individuals. You won't convince these trolls of your opinion, because they're not open to being convinced. Instead, you'll engage in a back-and-forth that will waste your time and exhaust your emotions. Let it go. Ignore it. And if seeing the comment on your site bothers you tremendously, you can always delete it. The blog is your platform, and you are the editor. The choice is your own.

Moms Know Best: When in Doubt, Think of Each Individual Reader

Jane Maynard started her blog, ThisWeekforDinner.com, to keep herself on track for meal planning and to get dinner ideas from friends. Weekly, she also shares recipes, kitchen tips, and gorgeous photos of food.

Q: What do you do with doubt?

A: Sometimes it's easy to get caught up in stats. Even the best of us have our moments. Whenever I start to get too focused on numbers, I step back and remind myself that's not what matters. I think about what my goals are and why I'm writing the blog in the first place. And I remember that whether you have ten readers or millions, each one of those "numbers" is a person on the other end, reading what you're writing and being impacted by it. I recently attended a conference for food bloggers. A woman with a successful blog came up to me, gave me a big hug, and said, "I credit you with the existence of my blog." She went on to tell me that reading my website had been her very first blog experience, and that her positive interaction with me had been a real inspiration. She was so sincere and so sweet that it did my heart good. Keep in mind that this is a person who rarely commented on my blog, but she was there reading it all the time, and in the end, my blog had a big impact on her life. She went on to blog herself, and it's opened up a whole new world of possibilities for her. When you're sitting in front of a computer screen, it's easy to feel disconnected. But the beauty of blogging is that it's all about people, and you really are connecting personally with the people reading your blog.

PACING

One topic we haven't raised yet but should—because it's the quickest way to burn out before you've got your groove on—is pacing. You've got to find the right pace for you, says Christine Koh of Boston Mamas. We agree. "It may take some experimentation, and that is okay; the point is that you want to find a balance where you aren't driving with the brake on. You want to feel joyful and inspired and excited about blogging, because that energy will come through in your writing. So, for example, when I started Boston Mamas, I was sort of crazy. I wrote about fifty posts before I launched for real, so that there would be enough for people to click around on when they got there. And then I posted three to five times per day, all while I was still holding down my full-time research job and had a baby at home. It was brutal. At some point I asked myself, *Why am I killing myself like this? It's totally taking the fun out of it.* So over time I stepped it back to posting twice a week on weekdays, and kept that pace for a while, and then as things got crazier and crazier (and we moved to a kindergarten schedule, which made afternoon posting more challenging), I decided to do one daily post (only deviating from that if something time-sensitive came up at the last minute), but seven days a week. No one seemed to complain, and I'm really happy with this schedule. Now I feel as if I can truly call myself a daily blog, and the pace is perfect for me right now."

No matter what your pace, you're not going to have the free time you once had (if you had any!) once you dive into this digital track seriously. It's consuming in the best way.

A Real Blog's Growth Chart: Colleen's ClassyMommy.com Story

Q: What did a week of blogging involve when you first started?

A: Oh, those sweet early days of my blog. So simple. So pure. I like to call it "A Post a Day Kept the Doctor Away." As a general rule, I posted just one "find" a day in the mom, baby, or kid category. It took between five and fifteen minutes maximum per day to actually write up the content. If I was feeling ambitious or especially excited about more than one product in one day and I had the time, I might post two items. How did I pick what to write about? No one was sending me a thing. I didn't see myself as Consumer Reports with a goal of doing stringent product testing or being scientific about anything. Instead, I wrote about whatever was top of mind.

My reviews were all based on either products I was using at home with my baby or cool finds I'd scope out and research while surfing the Internet, shopping at the mall, or reading magazines. I never thought about setting up an editorial calendar, but life and the seasons influence your writing regardless of who you are or what you're writing about. (Think of the magazines you read, featuring relevant seasonal and holiday finds at the appropriate times of year. I fell into that seasonal groove, too).

There were days when I wasn't sure what to write about, so I'd surf the online stores looking for cool products to feature. If I found a great online shop, I'd likely find ten or more items I loved, and I'd slowly feature all of them over the next few weeks.

There were no outside influences or distractions in the form of press releases landing in my inbox or requests from marketers to announce their newest product innovations. So those were the easy days. The only thing I had to worry about was keeping my blog alive. The goal I set for myself was one post a day. I missed this goal very rarely.

Q: When did ClassyMommy.com start to grow?

A: After six months, everything started ramping up. Suddenly I was getting emails asking for my address and if I wanted to review something. A network of mompreneurs had found my blog. In those early days there were very few mom blogs dedicated to reviewing products. Once one mompreneur had featured my review of her product on her site and displayed the "As Seen on ClassyMommy" badge, other mompreneurs then contacted me to promote their products. The cycle continued with each review, and more and more small businesses heard about Classy-Mommy.com. The mompreneurs and small business owners wanted free promotions or buzz, and they began sending me products to test out and review in the mom and baby category. If the product sounded like a fit for me and Mackenzie or Kyle,

I'd say, "Yes, please send, and I'll be sure to post." Once a week I'd get a package in the mail. How fun. It was like having Christmas in July.

Then before I knew it, that once-a-week package turned into three times a week. Each delivery made me feel a little more obligated to write about these "sent" items rather than just those I'd chosen myself. I began to pick and choose. I didn't cover items when I didn't like them or they just weren't newsworthy. There were too many things I did like; I couldn't waste a post on stuff that didn't pass muster.

The rule was still a post a day, and I added a giveaway per week, too. Sometimes I did videos of products, so people could get a real up-close and personal feel for my family and me and the products we were talking about.

It was about this time—eighteen months in—that I merged my personal blog (for my kids' pictures and family photos) with Classy Mommy, so that when cute family stuff happened, I shared it with all my readers. Those messy Popsicle faces and special moments from our family vacations at the beach or elsewhere gave the blog a more personal feel.

Q: Where are you today?

A: Almost five years in, everything feels exponentially faster and more intense—juggling content for posts, projects I'm involved in that were all made possible by the blog (conferences, spokesperson gigs, etc.), phone calls, travel, family, family, family. The busyness goes in cycles, but it's a constant wheel of action to keep up the site and maintain the household as a full-time mom.

My rule is still a post a day, but honestly there are days when I do nothing on my website. However, on some days I might post as many as ten times! I also continue to incorporate family photos about our own adventures and to run giveaways (at least once a week, as there are so many to offer, and my readers love them). In order to keep myself excited about the content I post—and in my efforts to expand—I've also added

Recall Updates, Family Travel, Celebrity Mom & Baby gossip, and movie reviews to the content I write about; it's a strategic fit with my Mom, Baby, and Kid product reviews. This content is also really easy to update, timely, and newsworthy.

So how do I do it all, you ask? I work during naps in the afternoon (one to two hours, depending on the day) and about one hour in the evening, and on Wednesdays I have a sitter all day, so I can really concentrate and bang out content.

Here's how the day goes now:

Wake up. Breakfast with the kids. Get everybody dressed. Quickly check Twitter, Facebook, and email for anything urgent or time-sensitive that needs to be handled. Check my Google alerts and feeds for all my hot keyword items, such as baby recalls or parenting news, so I can share pressing information with my readers on my blog, Facebook, and Twitter.

In the afternoon, create content, which means a daily product review, video, bit of celebrity mom gossip, and multiple giveaways, as well as pictures of the kids when we have them.

Some weeks now I receive a dozen or more items for us to play with and review. I don't come close to featuring everything I receive. I also probably hit delete on 75 percent of the PR pitches I receive, mostly because they're not relevant to my site's content.

I tend to write about whatever we like best at that moment. It needs to be different from anything I've recently posted about, too, so that I'm providing diverse content for readers. This spontaneity means that my to-do list gets reinvented daily, as products I like best or things I hear about on the web take priority over whatever my initial plan was.

And that's fine. I like being flexible. It works for me, and I keep it all a lot less like a job by doing what I want and not forcing anything. Sometimes I wish I had better predictability or a set editorial calendar. But I don't think that's my style. Writing product reviews daily is enough of a set plan.

Prioritizing is also now an important aspect of my day. My paid work often takes priority over unpaid work. And talking about a post on Twitter or Facebook sometimes means posting less new content. Every priority decision is carefully weighed: what's best for my readers, my family, and my income?

WE'LL KEEP SAYING IT: PERSISTENCE IS NECESSARY

So, have you done it? Have you hung your digital shingle yet? We hope so. And we hope you didn't pull it down on Day 3 or Month 3. So many do, and it's almost always right before they would have broken through to a wider audience. Success doesn't happen overnight. Patience is key. Yes, you need to keep writing regularly in those early days, even when basically no one but you, your best friend, and your goldfish are reading posts. But it pays off. We promise. In fact, here's where we tell you how to make the payoff come quicker.

Remember our list, "The Five Easiest Ways to Launch Yourself into the Digital Realm"? You might have thought, *Oh, I'll just pick one and really master it.* Well, what if we told you that the key to this whole business is actually picking all of them at once? The beauty of the web is that it loves to loop back on itself. So, for instance, if you've just launched a blog called A to Z Mom and a Twitter account by the same name, you can bet that fans from the blog will follow you to your Twitter account and back to the blog, too. If you launch under the same name at Facebook, well, you're basically broadcasting from three different stations at the same time. We call this multifaceted launch "hanging a 360-degree shingle." We both started with basic blogs, posting text entries with photos. Then we added videos to our blogs. Then we began posting on Facebook about our postings on our blogs. Then we found out who on Twitter might like what we were saying, and we began talking to them there. They followed us back to our blogs. We followed them back to theirs. Then to their YouTube pages, then to ours, then back to . . . You see where this is going? Our 360-degree shingle has brought us into a 360-degree world, filled with like-minded souls who enjoy what we have to say and vice versa. Can anything be more confidence building?

You should know that the web experts at the *Wall Street Journal* and the *New York Times* call this 360-degree shingle the first step in social networking. "Social networking" is a fancy term for making friends and alliances online through blogs, Twitter, Facebook, and the like. To us, "social networking" as a term sounds redundant and misses the finer details of what it's all about. In essence, hanging that 360-degree shingle means that you're visible at all the major social outposts on the Internet. This is crucial today, because people don't read only blogs or websites anymore. Instead, you need to find them where they are on the web, which is often hanging out on Facebook or Twitter.

So that means you need to be there, too. It's time to become a more active participant in the Digital Mom community, both online and offline. In the next chapter we'll talk all about making virtual friends and nurturing business relationships.

The relationships you form and the communities you join will give you reach, and with that newfound online presence, you can start thinking big. Real big. Thoughts like "I want 1,000 visitors to my next YouTube video!" And you know what? That may not be a far-fetched goal! So now that you've hung your digital shingle, get connected in **Step 3: Find Your Tribe.**

STEP 3

   Find Your Tribe

Call it a clan, call it a network, call it a family: Whatever
you call it, whoever you are, you need one.

—Jane Howard

I n the previous chapter we explained the 360-degree shingle. Once
you've got it up, a slow stream of traffic will start arriving at your door.
Of course, you could stop here, pat yourself on the back, and call yourself a
successful Digital Mom. And you know what? You absolutely deserve the pat.
But if you stop here, you'll miss what is perhaps the most rewarding aspect
of this whole Digital Mom venture (along with a whole lot more traffic to
your site).

Until now you may have been fairly passive on the networking front.
Have you actively and assertively sought out any online friends or mentors or
business associates? There's a whole community of women—many of them
moms like you—waiting to meet you, to help you take off and succeed. You
can't just stand still while traffic comes toward you. In Step 3 we want to get

you out of your comfort zone and actively seek specific people to follow and ultimately befriend. This step will require you to be discerning. It will also require you to find and engage the savvy online people who will become your offense, your defense, your champions, your virtual office mates, and your traffic drivers for as long as you shall live online.

It's time, in other words, to find your tribe.

WHERE AND HOW TO FIND YOUR TRIBE

Have you ever been to a networking event? Oh, my . . . they can be brutal, especially if you go alone. You stand around, making eye contact with random people, hoping to get a few good business cards by the end of the night. Networking online is a whole lot easier. You don't need to attend any meet-and-greets at night (say good-bye to missing bedtime with the kids!). You don't need to stand around passing out business cards. You don't need to make random small talk with people you have absolutely no connection with. And you don't even have to be in work clothes! You can be wearing pajamas, with your feet up on the couch. Sounds heavenly—right? Networking online is much easier and much more doable because it's on your time, and you decide where you want to go and be.

There are three basic steps to this process:

1. Keep posting and creating the content you're passionate about so that your tribe can come read it when you finally find them.

2. Start visiting and perusing other sites with similar audiences to your own site. These may be sites founded by moms who talk about the same topics you do or sell the same products. These moms may be from your area, or they may be women with whom you simply "click." Many women are looking to connect with other women who are going through similar experiences: adoption, infertility, having multiple children, breastfeeding, children with food allergies, ecofriendly living, and so on. There's something so special about finding women

in your same boat with whom you can be honest and open and candid. It's that connection and bond that forges the beginning of a beautiful and lasting relationship and friendship. (And, just because we haven't said so yet, you may even reach out to— gasp—men!)

3.   Send notes to the founders of the sites you're visiting; chat them up; compliment their sites. Inquire about guest posting and contributing. This is a major way to get your name out there and gain more traffic.

It all comes down to starting and joining in on conversations. Much like real life, right? But this won't be hard, because you're going to be sincere about it. You're going to visit only the sites that truly interest you, and you're going to send notes that express your true feelings about those sites. This is the informal meet-and-greet of online networking. It couldn't be easier, but it's amazing how many new Digital Moms forget to do it, don't understand the value of it, or are just plain afraid of it.

What are your goals in finding a tribe? Ask yourself these questions as you start out:

- Do you want to find people in your geographic area?
- Do you want to find other bloggers who write about what you do?
- Are you looking for friendships?
- Are you looking for strictly business relationships?
- Are you looking for a mentor?

Exploring in this way will introduce you to people through their words, photos, videos, and other creative forms. You'll quickly learn the names of their families, children, and pets. You'll also pretty quickly determine whom you truly enjoy checking in with, day in and day out, and whom you'd rather skip. Some people you will just "get" right off the bat. When you find them, it's incredible, like meeting a long-lost best friend.

Moms Know Best: Finding Out You're Found

Stephanie Precourt is a stay-at-home mom and freelance writer. Growing up, she had great plans to be on Broadway, in the movies, or directing children's theatre. Now she finds herself managing every type of drama, tragedy, and comedy within her little home in Valparaiso, Indiana. She has three small sons and a baby girl, so life is quite exciting and unpredictable—just without her name in lights. Stephanie journals daily about life and motherhood at Adventures in Babywearing (www.adventuresinbabywearing.com) and is a writer for *NWIparent Magazine* and the NWIparent blog Close to Home (www.nwitimes.com/parent/blog/closetohome).

Q: You started writing online in 2001 on Yahoo Geocities! after having your first son. Then you started a blog in 2005. You've been in this mom space for a long time. Tell us, how did people find you online, and who are daily check-ins for you?

A: Okay, to be honest, when I started blogging I didn't know there were other people writing stuff like mine. I used to sell my kids' clothes on eBay, and my first blog comment was from someone who had bought an item from me and had seen my blog listed in my "about me" page. She had a blog about motherhood, too (that is no longer around), and from there it was link after link. Someone would comment, and then I'd go comment on their blog. Before I knew it, there was this big beautiful community, and it was wonderful. The blogs that stick out in my mind as my first favorite blogs and mentors (and they are also blogs I still read faithfully to this day) are these:

Melodee at Actual Unretouched Photo
(www.actualunretouchedphoto.com)

Gretchen at Lifenut (www.lifenut.com/blog/)

Shannon at Rocks in My Dryer (www.rocksinmydryer
.typepad.com)

ENGAGING ON FACEBOOK AND TWITTER

Facebook and Twitter are not one-way streets. When in the active mode
of Finding Your Tribe, you need to think of these two huge communities—Facebook alone has surpassed 500 million users around the world,
as of July 2010—as a bit more dynamic than just bugles blowing in one
direction. For instance, if you've got a great blog post or an online store or a
big feature story to share, put it on your Facebook page and tweet about it
too. If you post on Facebook or Twitter, this announcement will appear on
your friends' feeds, it could get retweeted by friends, and suddenly, before
you know it, strangers will start arriving at your blog/store/story. And the
audience out there is considerable. According to BSM Media, 70 percent of
moms are on Facebook right now, and the number increases daily.

But better than that, if one of your friends—or even someone you
haven't met but would like to meet—posts her feature story or video blog to a
Facebook feed or Twitter, you should jump in and comment on it. It's a huge
missed opportunity if you don't. And nothing flatters a stranger more than
another stranger leaving a great comment. We view comments, whether via
blog, Facebook, and/or Twitter, as gold.

Twitter is great at helping us find like-minded moms because it has a
genius search mechanism that can find a needle in a haystack. In particular,
it can help you find other bloggers whose websites you like to read (and now
you can read their thoughts in 140 characters or less, which is probably all
you have time for, anyway). We're talking microblogging at its finest. Small
snippets and quick, fast information—believe it or not—are a great way to
get to know someone.

You can engage directly with these bloggers through the @reply command and begin to achieve a level of intimacy. In short, don't just make it about you, you, you. Ask questions, and definitely reply back and forth with others. If your Twitter profile doesn't have any level of engagement back and forth, chances are you're missing out on major opportunities to meet other people. Also, use Twitter to tweet out your blog postings via Tinyurl.com or Bit.Ly, websites that shorten your URL to help you include it in your 140-character tweet. This is a great way to get your content out to (literally) thousands and thousands of strangers.

GET YOUR PARTY ON AT A VIRTUAL CARNIVAL

A lot of new bloggers don't realize that mixers are going on all the time in the blogosphere—actual events invented solely for the purpose of getting bloggers to meet other bloggers. While they don't involve carousels and cotton candy, these mixers are often referred to as carnivals. The concept of a carnival in the blogosphere might be hard to visualize at first, but don't let that deter you. A carnival can help you expand your reach and ground yourself as an upstart blogger.

Essentially, a blog carnival is an event hosted by a major blog, like 5 Minutes for Mom (5minutesformom.com), which has been ranked the No. 2 family blog by the *Wall Street Journal* and formed partnerships with major companies such as Walt Disney World, Olive Garden, and more. In fact, the founders of 5 Minutes for Mom, twin sisters Janice Croze and Susan Carraretto, are the queens of blog carnivals. One of their most popular is called Wordless Wednesday, in which they give participants a basic prompt: post a photo to your blog—just a photo, no words. Some are funny. Some are serious. Some are very memorable—like a first haircut or a silly face. Anyone can be an active participant, because 5 Minutes for Mom posts links to every single blog participating in the carnival.

In this way, you're getting direct links to other great blogs, and other great blogs are being steered to you. You comment on these other blogs, the owners of those blogs comment on your sites, and voilà! More traffic for everyone. It's a great way to make virtual friends and connections and even get some free advertising. When Audrey started blogging in 2007, she participated in Wordless Wednesday every week and was introduced to hundreds of bloggers this way. The first Wordless Wednesday photo she posted was of her pregnant belly (with Benjamin), and she couldn't believe the response she got from so many bloggers! She was able to connect with bloggers who were also pregnant, and she connected with them instantly. It was such an easy and fun way for her to connect.

And Wordless Wednesday isn't the only carnival out there (though it sure is easy). There's Mingle Mondays, hosted at Eighty MPH Mom (www. eightymphmom.com), where participants record a video that answers a weekly question and publish it to their blogs, and Tackle-It Tuesday, another 5 Minutes for Mom creation, in which participants tackle something around the house that they've been putting off and share their success with other moms. Participating blog carnivals like these are nonintimidating and fun ways to connect with other bloggers by sharing your content, commenting on their websites, and vice versa.

JANICE CROZE AND SUSAN CARRARETTO'S FOUR TIPS FOR BUILDING AN AUDIENCE

1. Guest post and contribute to other sites. Not only does this bring traffic back to your site when people read your fantastic posts, but you are building powerful incoming links to your blog.

2. Write posts with Google in mind. Think about keywords and what people are searching to read. Title your posts accordingly. Consider using Google Trends (www.google.com/trends) to help you determine which keywords and topics people are most likely to use for a search.

3. Use social media! Not being on Twitter is social media suicide. A blogger must be on Twitter, and ideally Facebook and Linked In, at the minimum. When we started, we didn't have these tools at our disposal. Now they are integral to our promotion.

4. Most of all, play nicely with others! Remembering that the very lessons we teach our children on the playground also apply in the blogosphere will ensure that you are the kind of friend people want to make—and keep!

TWITTER PARTIES

Individuals also host mixers on Twitter, too (called Twitter parties). Twitter parties take place almost every night of the week. Hundreds of people come together at the same time to discuss the same topic, ranging from eco-friendly living tips to fashion trends to something as ordinary as new flavors of ice cream or innovative dish soap. No need to dress up in party clothes! Crash one, and you will find yourself communicating and sharing information with dozens, if not hundreds, of people in a series of fast and furious exchanges. To get yourself involved, we highly suggest you seek out Jyl Pattee of MomItForward.com and her Girls Night Out Parties (a.k.a. #GNO on Twitter), Amy Lupold Bair of ResourcefulMommy.com and her Sitewarming Parties, and Meghan Calhoun of SocialMoms.com.

Moms Know Best: When There's No Time to Blog, Tweet!

Alicia Ybarbo and Mary Ann Zoellner are TV producers; authors of *Today's Moms*, a book about surviving baby's first year; and avid tweeters.

Q: **While holding down big-time jobs for the No. 1 morning show in America, being moms, and writing a book, you still managed to successfully join the Digital Mom community as one of us. How did you do it?**

A: We tried blogging, but between having full-time jobs, two children each, and writing a book, we found that blogging just wasn't going to fit into that equation. To do so would have left us no time to make grocery lists and pack that snack for school, or simply to mentally unwind from a long day. As a result, we looked at Facebook and Twitter and made connections and friendships there. We've been lucky enough to build a large following on Twitter, even making Babble.com's list for Top Twitter Moms in 2010. We all have many things on our plates, but life is about editing your decisions in order to fit your lifestyle. Twitter is actually ideal for busy moms. Because of the limited character space you have to keep it short and sweet. Tinyurl.com is the greatest invention ever!

Q: **What tools helped you build your social media presence?**

A: We started off in my living room, hosting live events on Twitter and giving away free books and prizes. In March 2009 we became the second highest trend topic on Twitter. We did quite a few live Twitter events, and it was great to connect with other moms. We also hosted several social media parties, including one at NBC for our book launch. We invited the moms we connected with on Twitter and Facebook to that event, which was great.

Q: **Why was it so important to you to connect to the digital community?**

A: We all know it's a place where relationships are formed, but it's also a place of big business. Many moms have gone from sharing their overall parenting experiences online to narrowing down to one key area of focus such as cooking, photography, homeschooling, or home design. And as much as we all want to be successful and build our brand, it's also important to listen to the digital community. You can't just share what's going on in your world; you also need to pay attention to what the community is talking about. This is how friendships are made.

AM I FINDING MY TRIBE OR SPINNING MY WHEELS?

When you're spending time at all these online destinations, make sure you're gaining something from it. Moms have hectic schedules, and time is a precious commodity. When we're online, we need it to be beneficial—not to mention that usually our only downtime is in the early morning or the late evening.

You really (really!) want to see something good happening online, especially if you're trying to build a blog, a brand, or a business as a Digital Mom. We know—we've been there. It's only natural to wonder: what am I actually gaining from hanging out on other mom blogs, mom communities, Twitter, and Facebook? While you're looking for your tribe you may start to scratch your head a few times. And it's also natural for your husband (and possibly children) to ask the same questions and scratch their heads, too!

Colleen and Audrey's Five Tips: How to Tell if You're Making Progress

1. You're getting to know other women on a more personal and engaging level.

2. You're able to identify pretty quickly if you have the same likes and dislikes as a blogger you've been reading. This means you're definitely making the connection.

3.   You're finding someone online who blogs about the same things you do, and you can imagine a good partnership with that person (remember, there's power in numbers!).

4.   You've begun to find people you admire in the blogging world and have started following them on Twitter, Facebook, and any other social network you can.

5.   As a result of your efforts, you've seen some increases in traffic.

HOW TO MEASURE YOUR TRAFFIC

It's all about the numbers. Google Analytics is a must-have free tool you can install on your website to help you track key metrics like page views per month and unique visitors per month.

Also, get familiar with these additional different ways to evaluate your progress:

Alexa rank

Technorati rank

Twitter followers

Facebook fans

Klout score

YouTube subscribers

YouTube views

RSS readers

Moms Know Best: Moms Helping Moms

Kimberly Blaine, published author, vlogger, and founder of The Go To Mom and MommytoMommyTV, which offer online shows, has a lot of great advice to offer. Best of all, she gives it away for free. "I'll go to the ends of the earth for a mom who wants to improve or start her business," she says. But many new Digital Moms don't realize that they must give something in return for that advice, even if they feel they have nothing to give. "Established mompreneurs still enjoy and appreciate reciprocation. It feels good to be acknowledged. Showing appreciation to someone who has helped you could be a very big stepping stone in your career." It's as simple as promoting others, really. We've figured out the best ways to promote one another (and everyone else in our tribe) through trial and error.

Colleen and Audrey's Five Tips: How to Promote Others

Here's our list of surefire methods.

1. **Everyone loves a retweet on Twitter.** If someone you like tweets something that you feel could be beneficial to your followers, retweet it (a.k.a. forward it on). Suddenly you've spread one tweet far beyond its original reach.

2. **Give comment love.** Comment on blog posts, Facebook posts, Twitter posts, and LinkedIn status changes. Comment. Comment. Comment. It's a little of a time suck, yes; but if you commit

to commenting on ten sites a week, your tribe will love you for it and pay you back in spades.

3. **Video responses.** If you're into the video thing, consider creating video responses to published videos. It's like a comment but much more three-dimensional. Everyone will see your expressive face and really believe you.

4. **Content, content, content.** We're all looking for it, so give some to your tribal friends and make them ecstatic. It might take the form of an essay, a review, a video, or even a podcast. Conversely, integrate someone you like into your site. Interview someone, mention a post they've written, review a product they've reviewed, and give the credit. There are many ways to incorporate someone into a posting and subtly (or not so subtly) promote them.

5. **Don't overpromote.** This isn't brain science. If you're using too many exclamation points, if your comments don't reflect reality, or if you've left six complimentary posts in one day on the same subject, then you're overpromoting and will actually hurt your new friends more than you'll be helping them.

MENTORS CAN HOLD THE KEY TO SUCCESS

You also know you're finding your tribe when you stumble upon a seasoned Digital Mom—like Kimberly Blaine—who eagerly and earnestly wants to help you succeed. Colleen remembers the time she emailed Maria Bailey, founder of MomSelect, an organization that specializes in marketing to moms for many Fortune 500 clients, to ask for advice. Colleen was about to participate in a live satellite segment on Fox News discussing how the revised FTC guidelines could affect mom bloggers. It was a hot topic, and Colleen really didn't know if she should even agree to comment to the media. Colleen had never met Maria, a mom of four, and knew she'd be busy. But shortly after Colleen reached out, Maria was calling with advice and encouragement, telling her to definitely go on air, speak out, and share the voice of moms.

The day Colleen was on TV, Maria then tweeted and Facebooked about the segment again and again all day long, so everyone heard the buzz—classic mentor behavior. Sometimes mentors find you and sometimes you must seek them, but when seeking a mentor, look for someone like this:

- Someone who shares your interests

- Someone you feel comfortable asking for help

- Someone who understands your goals

The first point is so important, and finding someone who shares your interests should be easy. Communities abound on every topic from scrapbooking to weight loss to being pregnant with twins. And if you can't find a community out there that works for you on an existing site or message board section of popular sites for women like CafeMom, iVillage, Yahoo Shine or Baby Center, consider starting your own community.

Moms Know Best: What's in a Tribe?

Renee J. Ross, Cutie Booty Cakes

Q: You've been able to forge many strong tribes in the blogging space. How did it all begin for you?

A: In July 2008 I started a business targeted toward pregnant and new moms: diapers arranged to look like cakes. My blog initially began as a marketing tool for my Diaper Cake business, but soon after I started blogging I developed a love for sharing my life and learning about the lives of others. I quickly found blogging communities like the Mom Bloggers Club, Social Moms, MomDot, The SITS Girls, and PoshMama, and I started meeting as many people as possible.

Now, my online tribes are as important to me as my offline tribes. In the virtual world I can connect with members of the different tribes I belong to at any hour of the day or night. It's not realistic for me to call a friend in real life (IRL) at 3 a.m. if I'm suffering from insomnia, but with Twitter and Facebook, friends are just a tweet or status update away. I've found that many members of my online tribes have become my friends IRL, and I almost don't make a distinction between IRL and online anymore.

Q: How would you define the tribes you're in?

A: I'm a member of multiple tribes, and my involvement in them changes depending on my life. Currently I'm most active in the fitness community, but it's fluid. Fitness, mom, woman, Blog Her, African American—I am a member of all of these tribes, and I weave in and out of them seamlessly. In the blogging world, it was important for me to "meet" as many bloggers as possible. I wanted to see what worked well and what didn't. I read blogs in all different niches, even if I was not a "member" of that particular tribe. I believe we all have things that we can learn from each other, and by taking a multifaceted approach to blogging, I've had a vast array of experiences and touched all different types of people.

GETTING OUTSIDE

For all this discussion of Finding Your Tribe online, we're also telling you to put down your gadgets and walk out of the house. Why? Because now that you've found your tribe, it's time to meet in person, shake hands, look eye to eye, hug, and see if the relationship can go any further.

One of the quickest ways to meet a lot of common-minded online types at once is to attend a conference. Dozens have sprouted up in the past five years. While BlogHer is perhaps the largest conference for women bloggers in general, moms can seek out events like Blissdom, EVO Conference, Blogilicious, Type-A Mom, BlogWorld, BlogHer Food, Bloggy Boot Camp, Mom 2.0, and Disney Social Media Moms—and more new ones are popping up every year. It's likely that there are probably a few local social media club meetings in your city this week, too. Also, you can join many other incredible organizations that provide excellent platforms for professional women to network. Some of the following groups offer monthly meetings and/or annual conferences, and they also have websites that are full of information. NAWBO (the National Association of Women Business Owners), Ladies Who Launch, 85 Broads, and the Super Mom Entrepreneur Conference and Expo (founded by Lucinda Cross, the author of *Corporate Mom Drop Outs*) are just a few of the organizations that have been doing great things for women bloggers in recent years.

Conferences and meet-ups are an essential way to keep yourself relevant and in the loop. It's important to meet people face-to-face and allow your personality to shine through, past, and over your blog. There's nothing to be afraid of—we promise!

If you don't believe us, believe the mistress of meet-ups, Tiffany Romero. In 2008, after founding The Secret Is in the Sauce, a site designed to support women developing an online presence, Tiffany threw a live event, known then as SITScation, in Las Vegas. It was an intimate blogging conference that soon went viral. By 2009 she was hosting conferences similar to what is now known as Bloggy Boot Camp all over the country. They cost $100 and bought you a one-day intensive social media primer.

What more could we expect from a former camp director? "I wanted to provide an inclusive atmosphere that encouraged women to network in person," she told us. Attendees are introduced to a broad array of topics, including everything from SEO (search engine optimization) to social media etiquette to branding to writing. Speakers present for thirty minutes and then spend an additional fifteen to twenty minutes answering questions and interacting with the audience.

"While the education is top-notch and the attendees leave the event feeling motivated and ready to take their blog to the next level, the best part of Bloggy Boot Camp is the networking," Tiffany says. "Women often forge meaningful connections that lead to collaborations, support, and dialogue that continues long after the day is over. Meeting people outside of the computer changes things. It adds an authenticity to the relationships we develop online. It validates our endeavors, and I have created some of my most meaningful and supportive relationships with women I've met online. Having the opportunity to meet these women in person was, well, amazing. It's an experience I want women everywhere to have. The secret of success is support."

We certainly agree with that!

FROM PERSONAL EXPERIENCE: COLLEEN'S FIRST CONFERENCE

In the spring of 2008, Johnson & Johnson hosted a Camp Baby event for about fifty mom bloggers from across the country. I nervously left my four-month-old at home with Daddy and his two-year-old big sister while I drove two hours to North Jersey to meet up with the group. I fretted over what to wear and whether or not I would easily make friends. Honestly, I had been blogging for two years but had never met one person in my real life who spent time sharing her life online in the way I did. I truly did not know what to expect of the other attendees.

Within an hour of my arrival, I realized I had found my tribe. Regardless of what these women wrote about, they were passionate about sharing something online, and they lived and breathed blogging the way I did. It was invigorating and exciting to hear about their lives, their blogs, their past business experience or lack thereof, and their plans for the future of their websites.

Yes, there were cliques just like junior high, as some people had already been cyber friends for years, but those who had been lurking alone in their own online corner, like me, or were newer to the blogosphere, quickly formed their own friendly groups. For me it's the real-life connections that made everything tick online and cascade into future opportunities. I met someone on that trip who would end up hiring me a week later for a six-month consulting project. Incredible.

And I met Audrey's sister there, too (Audrey was at home, superpregnant with her fourth son). Little did I know that virtual introduction to Audrey would ultimately result in my finding a business partner, co-author, and online best friend. I never would have believed that within two years we would be meeting celebrities together, traveling around the country to work on campaigns, taking joint family vacations, or coauthoring a book to inspire other moms to find their inner digital selves.

After that meet-up, I was so invigorated. I knew I needed to find more local mom bloggers from Philadelphia. Within days of coming home from Camp Baby I organized a meet-up with Whitney from Mommies with Style, another online product reviewer. We had casually chatted online, but coincidentally we lived only ten minutes from each other. She's now one of my closest real-life friends and a business partner.

We talk on the phone every other day and see each other all the time. Our kids are even friends!

I started seeking out even more bloggers in Philly and quickly found out that Musings of a Housewife founder Jo Lynne Shane lives about fifteen minutes from me. Together we decided to throw a dinner with bloggers in the area. We posted on our sites to find people and got about thirteen attendees. After the success of our mom bloggers' night out at an Italian restaurant, we started an email Google list of Philadelphia-based bloggers. Since 2008, it's grown from about thirteen of us to more than eighty people, with more added weekly. The group now has a life of its own. It's a truly self-sustaining entity. The email list serves as a place for all these virtual people to exchange info, bounce questions off one another (especially if someone has a late-night tech crisis), invite one another to events, and just connect. This list and mom-to-mom networking has made Philly a hotbed of mom bloggers. Now brands and companies even approach us to host their events in Philly. And it all started because I made myself go to a conference I was nervous to even attend!

MIXING BUSINESS AND FRIENDS

Once you've found your tribe, the fun really starts. You go from flying solo to having collaborative partners to brainstorming new ideas and ventures. If you think you had a successful business before this moment, just wait. You'll find your tribe doing all sorts of things to benefit you and your burgeoning business, from linking to your site to talking you up to other popular bloggers, vloggers, and the like. The back-scratching is invaluable.

Now, within your tribe, there may be someone you really click with. Someone who stands out as, well, your digital best friend. A person you trust not only as a friend, adviser, and advocate but as someone you think you'd actually like to do business with. In fact, when you're feeling particularly tired and you've been on Twitter or Facebook for nine hours that day, advancing your digital career, you might even fantasize about this person sharing the burden of running this digital three-ring circus with you.

How do you think this book was made?

Now, before you team up with any person, you need to do some honest assessment—not just of yourself but of your potential partner and partnership. Are you a team player? Is your friend? Does she/he motivate and push you, and vice versa? Could you freely discuss money with this person? Do you have the same expectations and work ethic? Do you have a similar communication style (said another way: will she/he embarrass you in front of others with awkward emails and conference calls?).

On paper, we were a perfect match, from our educational backgrounds to our professional drive to our corporate experience. We were certain we'd make a great team, but we needed to make sure our business expectations were aligned, so we each made a list and put our lists side by side. What did she want; what did I want? And where did our wants intersect?

Colleen's List

Make money with my time
and hard work

Be at home with my children

Write a book

Be on camera

Find spokesperson opportunities

Audrey's List

Make money with my time
and hard work

Be at home with my children

Write a book

Be on camera

Find spokesperson opportunities

To say that we intersected would be an understatement!

By interviewing other teams like ours, we've learned that this intersection isn't so uncommon. We wanted to make money together; we wanted to merge our traffic streams to build one giant traffic stream; we wanted to have someone to lean on for confidence; we wanted cross-promotion; and we wanted to be able to approach companies like Healthy Choice, Tide, and Kodak with a united front. A small mommy retailer might also want a partnership like ours, though the reasons and outcomes might be different. For instance, two small retailers working together might be able to present more products, have a deeper inventory, afford better e-commerce technology, and merge traffic streams. If there's one truth we have found working with different brands and companies in the blogosphere, it's that there's power in numbers.

Here are some of the key benefits of teaming up with another blogger:

1. **Accountability.** You're less likely to drop the ball when you're accountable to someone besides yourself.

2. **Leverage.** You can double your fee in certain circumstances (such as when a company approaches you for assistance or consultation).

3. **Bigger audience.** You inherit not only each other's traffic but the traffic of each other's tribes.

4. **Better brainstorming.** There's always an additional head working, which means double the ideas and creativity.

5. **A confidante.** We can't tell you how meaningful it is to be able to bounce questions, problems, and confidential information off someone you trust.

Our first cooperative project together was in 2009. We had just come back from the South by Southwest (SXSW) conference in Austin, Texas, and while there, we met the marketing team behind Healthy Choice. Now we are both huge fans of Healthy Choice products, and we are the first to admit that we aren't the best in the kitchen. Needless to say, we saw an opportunity to show the company our collective love after the friendly intro at SXSW. And if we impressed them, we thought (fantasized) that the company might hire us to help with its future marketing efforts.

Not knowing how to pitch ourselves, we turned to a PR professional whom we knew well. She told us to pitch three different campaigns: basically videos with different themes that cost different amounts to produce, one valued at $10,000, one at $5,000, and one at $1,500. So talking on the phone and emailing a dozen times a day, we put together a storyboard (we didn't know what a storyboard was until that moment) and laid out all of our ideas for a six-week video campaign. Healthy Choice accepted our $10,000 idea, which just sent the two of us into overdrive. If we were talking on the phone three times a day for the pitch, we were now talking ten times a day to prepare the videos. Each of us had to produce eight videos, with complementary ideas and themes. We couldn't afford to mess up our first big project together! Fortunately, we both have the same work ethic, which is one key to our success. Also, we're each willing to take on a greater share of the work when the other is especially busy—no questions asked. In the end, whether we need to step up for our partner, honor a family obligation, care for sick kids, or pursue an urgent business opportunity, it all balances out. We complement each other beautifully and, as a result, really enjoy our partnership.

The best part about it all? We had each other at the end of the day, and we had so much fun together. Bottom line: if you can't imagine this much together time with a business partner, then it's better to work alone.

Moms Know Best: Love at First Comment

Liz Gumbiner, of Mom-101.com, and Kristen Chase, Motherhood Uncensored, partners and founders of Cool Mom Picks and Cool Mom Tech.

Here's what Liz has to say:

Our partnership is a real Internet love story—we met online through our personal blogs; Kristen was already the popular author of Motherhooduncensored.net, and I had just launched Mom-101.com. She was the blogger of the week in this blog ring we were in, so I left her a note of congrats and she (gasp) deigned to leave a comment back. It was love at first comment.

Kristen has always been an incredible community leader in the mom blogosphere and shortly thereafter, she had the idea for a website called Cool Mom S***, which featured cool things we were finding online that mom bloggers were making or doing. She asked me and a few other contributors to join her and write some posts. My mind started reeling with possibilities, and I asked if she wanted to go in on it as partners, and she shockingly accepted.

Our first joint decision was to change the name to Cool Mom Picks, which had a little less baggage—and also didn't look like "Cool Moms Hit" in the URL! I will admit I did go into it with some healthy skepticism; I had never met Kristen in person, and in the past, I've had some challenging partners on various projects. I was hoping that she was as trusting and giving as she seemed to be, and as it turned out, she is. In fact, I couldn't ask for a more incredible partner. I remember asking, "Are you sure it's okay that I tweaked your headline?" And she'd say, "Of course! Whatever you think!"

I think the relationship works in part because we have a tremendous amount of mutual respect for each nother's taste, sensibility, and commitment to the site. She lets me edit her posts, and I let her veto my picks. We leave our egos at the door with Cool Mom Picks. I trust Kristen without hesitation about anything at all. If I can't be around, she'll always be there to step in for me, and vice versa.

That's particularly important. As working moms, we cover for each other and allot for work–life balance (to whatever degree that's possible). When one of us is having a tough time at home for any reason, taking vacation, or experiencing demands on our time from other projects, we're always willing to step in for the other. In close to five years of working together, we've never had a talk about "who does more." I think we both believe that it all evens out over time. Let's just say we're both the type who divides the check down the middle, instead of saying, "Well, you had the salad and I had the wine but I didn't get a dessert."

We also haven't had any distance challenges, even though I'm in New York City and Kristen is in Atlanta. As much as I'd love to have her here, with all the incredible technology available to us, I feel like we're in one office with two floors. When people ask where we're based, I always answer, "the Internet."

ARE WE DONE YET?

So you've found your tribe and forged alliances, secured a mentor, and possibly even launched a partnered venture with your new online bff. This is cause for celebration. And yet, you still have no income to buy the wine and streamers. Yes, here we are at the end of Step 3, and we still haven't uttered the word we know you've been thinking to yourself this whole time: money. Where is it? How do we make it? Who gives it to us? How can all this talking, tweeting, commenting, attending conferences, and so on ever lead to earning a dime?

Hold tight. We're getting there. **Step 4: Make Opportunity Knock and Learn How to Answer That Door** is next. But if you had skipped to it before reading and mastering Steps 1, 2, and 3, it wouldn't have had the most impact. It's sort of like eating dessert before you've finished dinner. Just a friendly warning from us moms!

STEP 4

Make Opportunity Knock and Learn How to Answer That Door

Here's the scenario: let's pretend there was a fictional mom named Jessica who launched a blog called BabyHatsBack.com. She started it on a lark. She was a knitter and a terrific seamstress, and she loved to make hats for her fair-haired sons in California. At first, the site was just a great place to feature photos of the kids in her hats. Friends and relatives showed up and sent her glowing comments. "The hats are fabulous. Send me one. I'll mail you a check for $20." "Make more babies. You've got the genes, Jessica!" Jessica loved all this feedback. She was alone at home with her three sons, and any contact with the outside world felt thrilling. She did her blog uploads while the boys napped or at night when her husband was watching football; she happily neglected the dirty dishes in the sink.

As time went on, Jessica drew more and more traffic. She posted more pictures and wrote longer posts. The hats became secondary to her great posts. People just loved to read about her quirky family, her philosophy of life, and her rants about all things related to public school—lice, bullies, and so on.

In the wee hours, she started vlogging, her husband holding the Flip camera for her while she knitted and joked with her fans. Traffic grew. Her mentor, another knitter/blogger, encouraged her to start using Twitter and Facebook to expand her reach further.

A year after launching, Jessica and her mentor started working together to produce funny videos that showed them knitting and joking about all things family related. They formed a new site called sittingandknitting. Their videos went viral on YouTube: 10,000 clicks on average!

Jessica thought these developments were really exciting. She would have told anyone who asked that this was her happily-ever-after story—she could spend time with her kids, knit, and spout off about anything that made her laugh or annoyed. She had a trustworthy business partner and fans who loved her.

And then Jessica received a very cryptic tweet from a man working for Company X, which specialized in luxury goods. His short communiqué read, "Be a spokeswoman for us, in Paris?" Jessica tweeted back. "I think you've got the wrong gal." A second later the man replied, "Nope, I've got the right gal." Jessica looked around for someone to grab and squeeze, but all she could see were sleeping babies and an overheated sewing machine. This must be a mistake, she thought. He must have mistyped. Maybe he meant to write "Be a pokey person"? That's the sort of nonsense she'd come to expect from Twitter. But spokesperson? Come on. Those jobs were for movie stars and guys like Joe Montana! Had he seen her thighs? This must be a giant mistake, she thought. But what if it wasn't?

Are you scratching your head, too? Are you asking

1. Why is a blogger like Jessica being offered a spokesperson job in Paris?

2. What exactly is involved in a spokesperson job for a gal like Jessica?

3.   Who would be insane enough to turn down such an offer?

Good questions, all. And to answer them, we must begin with a little economy lesson about moms, spending habits, marketing, and the reach of the Internet.

As you know, moms are typically the spenders in the household. We grocery shop, we buy clothes for the kids, and we often handle bills and banking. So it's no surprise that, according to the 2009 Women and Social Media Study by BlogHer, iVillage, and Compass Partners, $0.82 of every dollar spent in the United States is by women. No wonder advertisers want to influence every mom's purchasing decision. And no wonder they're going to the Internet to do it. According to a recent eMarketer report, moms are all over the Internet: some thirty-three million this year and climbing. And

- 54 percent of online moms visit blogs each month.

- 3.9 million women with children under eighteen write blogs.

- 51.1 percent of moms use Facebook to tell their friends about a product.

- 27.8 percent use their blogs to tell others about a product.

So, if moms are the major spenders, and moms are all over the Internet, how are advertisers reaching them? Through Digital Moms—moms with blogs and massive Twitter and Facebook followings; moms who are persuasive and trustworthy; moms who are smart, savvy, and entrepreneurial with a natural ability to influence others. Moms like us. Moms like you.

Advertisers see your blog as a giant microphone. It gives you a voice and a platform where you can share your opinion—your real opinion, whether it's just your opinion about your child's night waking routine, the fabulous deal you found on Halloween costumes, or the stellar chocolate soufflé you made for that dinner party last weekend.

If you're new to blogging, you might be thinking that your little blog seems too tiny to be worth much to an advertiser. At first glance that's probably true, but like all real estate, it does have value, and its worth generally increases over time—especially if you make the improvements we recommend. Whether you have 500, 50,000, or 5 million visitors a month, the point is that every single one of those visitors has the ability to purchase something, and you have the ability to influence that purchasing decision through your content.

Let's get more specific now. Every major (and minor) company— think Target, Baskin-Robbins, Subway, and so on—has a marketing budget. With that money, the company might buy ads in a magazine or newspaper, purchase and produce a TV commercial, buy a billboard on the side of a turnpike, or buy a radio spot. Or for much, much less money, they might try to find a blogger or vlogger to do their product proselytizing for them.

The truth is, online voices like ours and other sites with decent traffic are a boon to marketers and public relations firms. We've made their jobs *so* much easier. Why? Because when they convince us to run one of their ads on our sites, or get us to review one of their products in a vlog, or feature news about their company on our Twitter or Facebook pages, we're doing the job—practically for free—of a $1 million dollar TV ad or billboard or radio spot. In fact, we're often doing it better than the expensive ads because we're sharing our real experiences, which people generally tend to relate to far more than they would to a fifteen-second TV commercial. We provide honest mom-to-mom interaction, the good and the bad of an experience, and we're not commercials (most of us). Even better, bloggers are fast. While it takes months to produce a TV or radio spot, get coverage in a magazine, or obtain a prime billboard location, it takes only minutes to post a review of a new detergent or share news about the latest toy trend.

To repeat, marketers dangle prizes in front of us so that we'll consider doing their bidding because

1. We are cheap.

2. We are authentic.

3. We have a devoted readership that happens to be the exact demographic that the company needs to reach.

OPPORTUNITY KNOCKING

Like so many of you, we'd been going about our business when suddenly a prize fell from the sky. Well, more accurately, the verbal promise of a prize fell from the sky.

We've seen this happen time and time again. These prizes can take many forms:

- Swag (a free bicycle, a free toy, a vacation to Bermuda)

- An invitation to speak at an event on behalf of a company in a swanky location

- An opportunity to consult for a company and receive an ongoing stream of swag

- Tickets to a major event (the Oscars, the World Series, the Olympics)

- A free Louis Vuitton or other unthinkably expensive item

- A chance to simply own or do something you'd never dreamed possible

- Money (though it's the least likely)

The first reaction to such an offer is almost always "Yes! I'll take it. I'll do it! Where do I sign?!" We're hardwired for yes. We not only want the prize but feel we deserve it. All our hard work is paying off, we think. It's human nature not to consider the consequences beforehand—or ever.

Too true. And too dangerous. As a Digital Mom you're going to have to exercise some self-control. In fact, this is a pivotal moment in your life as a blogger. A moment in which we must remind you what we said in the Introduction: you determine your own version of success. No spokesperson gig or swag offering determines that for you.

Read on to learn more about these opportunities, including when to say yes and when to say no, and how to say yes and how to say no.

STRINGS ATTACHED

With the above introduction to online marketing under your belt, you are now empowered, discerning, and wise. But we have a lot more to talk about. Just because a marketer might offer you something doesn't mean you need to take their innovative gadget or free sample of honey, toothpaste, or some other product and post about it on your blog. Why might you say no to a lifetime's supply of tennis balls, getting your bathroom remodeled for free, a trip to the circus, or a seat next to Patrick Dempsey at the Oscars? Because often there are strings attached to that dangling prize.

If you do say yes to opportunities, know that companies or PR firms are offering you these perks with the hope that they'll gain a coveted post or a press mention on your blog or site. In the ideal world, if Ralph Lauren sends Audrey and Colleen a free sweater, RL will likely end up with a post or tweet commenting on their new sweater styles. Whether the review is good, bad, or even ugly, it generates some valuable "word of mom" buzz.

Moms Know Best: You're Worth More Than Free Yogurt

Amy Clark, the founder of momadvice.com, recently wrote a post called "I Did It My Way: Long-Term Blogging Success Tips" and told us that we could excerpt anything we wanted from it for our book. Bless her. This was our favorite piece of advice:

Free stuff is often one of the perks that bloggers get most excited about. As someone who was watching her spending, it was something I was very enthusiastic about when I started. Here's the thing I wish someone had told me: "Your blog is worth more than a carton of free yogurt."

I use free yogurt only as an analogy, but I'm saddened at how many seem to compromise their blogging space for free stuff. I would encourage you to really think about what your time is worth and select opportunities that are really worth the time you're spending on them. Focus your efforts on the things that promote your passions and that will benefit your community.

This means you have to turn down opportunities; it means you will be overlooked for trip opportunities; it means you might not be able to receive a paycheck from a company. You know why all that is okay? Because your readers will respect you. And that's worth more than a free yogurt, more than a trip, and even more than a paycheck. It is that loyalty that will help your community grow and will translate into paid opportunities that do fit you.

It's sometimes been hard to turn stuff down. I had an opportunity to do my grocery shopping for free, but they wanted me to showcase convenience foods you could buy to start the school year off right. A stocked fridge would have been great, but would you have respected me for telling you to buy crap food to stock your freezer to get your kid's day started out right?

This is not an exclusive opportunity. I get something like that in my inbox all of the time. I refuse a lot of it because I respect your opinion more than a corporation's opinion. It means I have moved to the D list for a lot of invitations and parties, but I hope I made the A list for my readers!

Remember, you don't need to write about every sample that might come your way or accept every gig dangled in front of you by a public relations company. You might not be the *New York Times*, but you are a business-woman who needs to make smart editorial decisions about the content you post. "If you can't feature a product because you didn't care for it or it didn't fit your criteria, that's okay. Don't feel bad about it. We need that feedback," says Heather Bandura, a PR specialist who works with bloggers, hoping they'll say great things about her clients but knowing they sometimes won't or can't.

There are also practical matters that may force you to say no:

Colleen and Audrey's Five Reasons to Say No

1. You may love a product or company, but if the company and its products have no relationship to your site, then you should probably say no (e.g., Audrey writes about fashion, beauty, and being the mother of four boys, so you won't find her helping companies that are focused on horseback riding or raising daughters).

2. There may be travel involved that you don't have the time for.

3. The company may want you to cover an event in New York City or Los Angeles, but they're not willing to foot the bill to get you there.

4. The company may be asking everyone in your tribe to plug their products, making you feel like a bit of a shill.

5. You have no desire to align yourself with any company, ever.

So there are many reasons to say yes and just as many to say no. We can't tell you whether or not a particular opportunity is right for you. However, we can certainly help you figure that out for yourself. Before responding to any request, ask yourself these questions:

• What will this do for my site? Will covering it lead to great added content, including videos, photos, and interviews?

- Is it contrary to my beliefs?

- If I write about it, will my readers like it or hate it, trust me more or less?

- Is it a paid opportunity, and do I need the money?

- If it requires travel, how long will I be away from my family? Can I bring my family with me?

- Thinking long term, what could come from this opportunity?

- Am I the only person being offered this opportunity, or one of a thousand?

- What will the company do to promote me, and will it improve my traffic?

THE UPSIDE OF SAYING YES

Aside from the obvious reasons to say yes—the stuff, the trip, the feeling of importance, the access to people and places you might never have access to again—some other bonuses can come along with saying yes that you might not be aware of.

1. **Referrals**. One opportunity usually leads to others. If you prove you're good at batting for a company—that you're fast, even-handed, and know how to sell without overselling to your readers— you'll be approached again, either by the same company or by another that has heard about your abilities in this marketing arena.

2. **Better brand recognition.** By being on TV or in front of a microphone as part of a company's marketing campaign, you're expanding the reach of your brand. You're getting exposure you might not otherwise have.

3. **A fuller Rolodex.** You might meet other bloggers or VIPs worth staying in touch with, who can either expand your brand or

open an opportunity to you later. In essence, you may gain a very valuable connection for later use.

WHO MIGHT KNOCK

The folks dangling carrots in front of us usually take the form of public relations professionals. They work with the brands and companies, and they typically choose the Digital Mom (or person) for opportunities, or at least recommend a very short list. The brands and companies rely on these recommendations. They're looking for solid, reliable, hardworking Digital Moms.

As in any field, there are great PR people and not-so-great ones. The great ones will actually visit your site, read or watch your posts, and even comment on your ideas before making a formal introduction. The not-so-great ones will make offers before they even know who you are or what you're about. The great ones will engage you, ask you questions, and really want to know you. The not-so-great ones will seem like snake oil salesmen.

Audrey will never forget the first PR person she became friendly with: Gillian Kushner from Weber Shandwick. They met in New York City in February 2009 at one of renowned social media expert Jeff Pulver's 140 Conferences. Gillian had reached out to Audrey a couple of months before to have her help with a campaign for one of her clients. Audrey liked her immediately because she wasn't sending out copy-and-paste pitches (the kind in which about 5000 women receive the same one). And Audrey could tell that Gillian had actually been to her blog. She knew that Audrey had four sons, and she even knew some of the blog postings. These are the kind of PR people you want to be working with. And as they're trying to sell you and your blog to one of their clients, you know that they're doing the best possible job for you, because they know you.

We interviewed a few of our favorites so you can hear how they think and what they're looking for in a Digital Mom.

Professional Advice for Bloggers from Public Relations Experts

Sarah Pasquinucci of Procter & Gamble External Relations North American Fabric Care.

Q: How does a company as big as P&G find valuable bloggers to create relationships with?

A: There are so many factors that make a blogger valuable and influential. It isn't about a blogger's reach but about whom they reach. These bloggers might reach a large number of consumers, but do they reach the right consumers? They might be influential among connectors, traditional media, or true brand advocates. These all play a role in making a particular blogger or blogger network influential.

Q: How do you successfully compel bloggers to write about your brands—something as simple and basic as laundry detergent or fabric softener?

A: We focus on giving the bloggers the content they need to serve their readers. It might be exclusive content, a unique experience, or a peek behind the curtain.

Q: How can bloggers build successful relationships with brands?

A: What makes bloggers a bit unique from traditional media is their personal touch. It is important that bloggers know their readers, and serve their

readers first and foremost. With that deep understanding comes the understanding of what brands
are relevant to both the blogger and his/her following. Never compromise who you are or what
you stand for in order to work with a brand. Brands
want a true influencer who is authentic and has the
trust of their readers.

*Angelica Colantuoni, Vice President of Digital,
Weber Shandwick*

**Q: Can you share tips that will help bloggers
working with PR professionals?**

A: Do your research. If you have specific companies
you would like to work with, do some digging to
find out who does their PR, and directly contact
them to express your interest in working with
them. A quick Google search will uncover any recently distributed press releases that list PR contact
names, as well as their contact information. Also,
do research to see where these brands are online.
Do they have a Facebook page? Are they on Twitter? After you've done so:

1. **Introduce yourself.** Any good PR professional will welcome
   emails, phone calls, or introductions at events and blogger
   conferences. Don't be shy. We're looking for people who are
   a great fit for our clients.

2. **Develop personal relationships.** As with any business, networking and developing personal relationships goes a long

way. This doesn't mean that you have to develop a personal relationship with every PR person that exists, especially if you don't click! You only need to get to know a handful of PR professionals whom you like and respect, and who have a good network. The PR industry is really a small world, so if your contact doesn't have a direct connection to the brand you want to work with, they most likely know someone who does.

3. **Be professional.** As with any business relationship, follow through on obligations, and maintain open and honest communications.

4. **Stay true to who you are.** A good PR professional will not be offended if you say no. They will appreciate your honesty and transparency, and so will your readers.

Lisa Orman, owner of Kid Stuff PR

Q: Bloggers wonder how to get noticed by PR firms. How do you decide which bloggers to offer campaigns or send press releases to?

A: We look for a combination of stats/readers/views/ visitors, so be ready with those, but also a personal style in reviews that goes beyond pasting in a press release and includes your own photos and/ or videos. All of this brings a personal note to the review, and that's what bloggers bring to the table versus traditional media outlets that are supposed to remain "objective." You may not have a million readers the way a magazine does, but if your

10,000 readers believe what you write and feel a connection to you, that's worth a lot to publicists and their clients! My pet peeve with bloggers is the few who take a sample for review and then disappear, don't reply to follow-up emails, or take months to post their review with lots of nagging. No thanks!

DISSECTING A PRESS RELEASE

If you're going to be part of this media arsenal, then you need to learn how to read its signals like all the other professionals out there. And press releases are one of the major signals you're going to get.

In the past, press releases went strictly to mainstream media outlets—TV news, newspapers, magazines—but now the web is littered with them. A release is a company's quick and easy way to announce something and elicit a response—hopefully from you, the woman with the traffic. And that response, they hope, will take the form of a post. So, for instance, what do you do if you receive a press release from Old Navy announcing a twenty-four-hour sale on denim and outerwear in every store across the country? Old Navy is hoping you will write, vlog, podcast, tweet, or otherwise talk about this, because they want all your readers running to Old Navy to drop big bucks. But you have to think twice before you do anything. Yes, the press release is your signal to release the "news" to your readers. But should you? Since you will undoubtedly see a press release in your inbox in the near future, here a few tips for dissecting it and weighing the pros and cons of "releasing" what's being pressed on you:

- Is the product/event the press release is talking about something you would actually use/go to? Or is it information that could benefit your readers?

- If it's in regard to a product review, are they offering to send you something to review, and are you interested in that something?

- Did the PR company address you by name in the email when they sent the press release? Or were you "Dear Mommy Blogger?" If the latter, feel free to ignore, since you're being treated as one in a million.

- In general, are you comfortable blogging about this?

To help you understand press releases, let's take a look at the way two different companies reached out to us recently. Although both provided perfectly acceptable releases, see if you can figure out why one commanded our attention while the other did not.

This first release showed up in our inbox unsolicited and without introduction:

News Release
GET RID OF SNAKES WITH SWEENEY'S
SNAKE REPELLENT
New All-Natural Repellent Is Safe to Use Around Children, Pets, and Gardens

ST. LOUIS—March 25, 2010—Sweeney's, the country's leading producer of pest control products for consumers, has added an all-natural, biodegradable snake repellent to its product lineup. Ideal for use around swing sets, sandboxes, pools, gardens, sheds, and woodpiles, Sweeney's Snake Repellent granules are easily applied anywhere you want to repel snakes.

"Snakes continuously monitor their surroundings by 'sensing' chemicals from the air with their tongues," explains Stew Clark, Director of Research and Development at Sweeney's. "Sweeney's Snake Repellent emits a sweet, pungent aroma that snakes find distasteful, causing them to leave the area without harming them."

That one was most unexpected for ClassyMommy! But here's one that really is a natural fit. Notice also that instead of just emailing a press release, the PR rep also sent a personal note. The human touch always helps!

> Hi Colleen,
> Today, Toys "R" Us, Inc. made two exciting announcements that might interest your readers:
>
> FAO Schwarz unveiled a brand redesign that will be translated throughout all its offerings, beginning a new chapter in the nearly 150-year-old legendary retailer's storied history.
>
> Toys "R" Us announced it will help make it easy for customers with older iPod models to purchase new iPods during the company's first-ever iPod trade-up program. Taking place in more than 550 Toys "R" Us stores across the country, customers can find extra value in their used music players—up to $100—when they trade in their previously used, working iPods from Sunday, October 17, to Saturday, October 23.
>
> Please see below for further details and feel free to contact me with any questions.
>
> Best,
> XYZ PR representative at Toys "R" Us

What followed the email from Toys "R" Us was a detailed press release that went into considerable detail about FAO Schwarz's redesign and the iPod trade-up program. While our impulse would usually be to skip long releases, the way we were engaged made all the difference.

Common courtesy and good manners used to mean we needed to respond to every opportunity in our inboxes, but we've hardened over time. As good as they are to us, those marketers are being paid to do all their emailing, and we're not. Today we have one finger hovering over the delete key at all times, working hard not to feel guilty about hitting it. In short, if you aren't feeling the vibe from the press release, don't hesitate to get it out of your inbox. (Alternatively, save the email in case, six months from now, you decide to reach out to the PR firm that sent it.)

UNPAID CAREER OPPORTUNITIES FOR THE DIGITAL MOM

Free popcorn, free socks, free DVDs of new TV shows, fogless mirrors, family vacations to all kinds of destinations, free circus tickets, and free trips to Disney on Ice. The Oscars, People's Choice Awards, Fashion Week, MTV awards, BET awards. Patrick Dempsey, Holly Robinson Peete, Tori Spelling, Melissa Joan Hart, Molly Ringwald, Melina Kanakaredes, and Chandra Wilson. Our Digital Mom gigs have given us access to all these items, places, people, and more. It's a wide world of endless opportunities. Since these "opps" are what our readers tell us they want to hear about most, we think they deserve a bit more attention:

Press junket reporter: A trip paid for by a company to show off its wares and give Digital Moms compelling content to take home and write about.

Activities and responsibilities: Honda invites Digital Moms to test drive the new Honda Odyssey. Frito Lay invites Digital Moms to company headquarters to see its snack-making factory operations.

Pros: These trips often provide very interesting content to share with your readers and are excellent networking opportunities for you to interact with brands and other bloggers. Child care is often reimbursed if you ask for it at a set rate between about $100 and $250/day.

Cons: These opportunities are almost never paid and require you to travel. Typically with traveling you'll be gone at least twenty-four hours, if not seventy-two. The content may or may not be relevant, depending on what you blog about regularly.

Compensation: Travel and hotel expenses. Possible swag bag of company products.

Celebrity interviewer: An opportunity extended by a brand or a TV network to meet a celebrity—by phone or in person.

Activities and responsibilities: Pack 900 snack boxes for Save the Children with Jennifer Garner; meet Molly Ringwald for lunch over Ragú travel to Hollywood to see a prescreening of a movie and then attend a parent blogger roundtable with the stars of the film; do a conference call with Patrick Dempsey, Melissa Joan Hart, Soleil Moon Frye, or a handful of other celebs. Whether we actually like the celebrity in question and whether a charitable tie-in exists tend to affect our reply.

Pros: Phone interviews last about ten minutes, and the studio will usually send you a video clip of your interview to embed on your blog. If you travel to meet a celebrity, the photos are fabulous and make for great content.

Cons: If you have to travel to an event, it may disrupt your child care routine.

Compensation: Travel expenses are typically compensated.

Product reviewer: In exchange for a review, companies mail you free stuff.

Activities and responsibilities: Covering products like iPhones, kitchen appliances, clothing, cars, and playsets. Time to review can range from ten minutes (if the review is of a new flavor of Popsicle) to three months (if it's reporting back weekly on how you like your new Frigidaire appliances).

Pros: You often get to test out things before they hit the market, and it's fun to be in the know before your friends! Kids also love having toys their friends have never heard of.

Cons: You'll spend a lot of time unpacking boxes, answering emails, and sending your links to the companies if and when you post a review. Also, if you don't like a product and decide it doesn't merit attention on your blog, you might need to consider letting the company know your feedback.

Compensation: Paid in product or a gift card to shop at a specific store.

Unpaid brand ambassador: An unpaid arrangement with a company to post about its product(s).

Activities and responsibilities: Maintaining a relationship with a company in which you, as the blogger, agree to have a long-term relationship with the brand. For example, Audrey received a free swing set for her boys from Backyard Discovery Toys when she agreed to be an unpaid brand ambassador for the company and post about her experience with the swing set. Both of us are members of the Hanes Comfort Crew, and we share product buzz and giveaways with our audience on an ongoing basis. We also share feedback with Hanes as needed.

Pros: It's a great résumé builder and aligns your blog or business with a brand. It's a great way to build strong relationships with the PR team or brand managers.

Cons: The only con is that you're working for free, which takes away time from your family and your other paid opportunities.

Compensation: Paid in product.

Speaker: An opportunity to speak in front of an audience in a conference setting.

Activities and responsibilities: Participating in a panel discussion to share your expertise and opinion, or preparing your own presentation on a topic, complete with PowerPoint slides.

Pros: These opportunities offer you a chance to gain credibility in front of your peers (if it's a blogging conference).

Cons: Speaking usually requires prep time (to write your speech) and travel time (one to three days, depending on location). Also, the gig is typically unpaid.

Compensation: Travel and expenses. The conference fee is waived, so you can attend for free.

Travel writer: An all-expenses-paid trip to a very compelling destination, such as a five-star resort, in exchange for posts about your trip.

Activities and responsibilities: Attending a Disney cruise or taking trip to Sea World just for moms, or a Carnival Cruise for the whole family; writing reviews and profiles of the destinations you visit.

Pros: These trips are gold if you're able to bring your family with you. If you must go alone, it's not exactly torture.

Cons: If you can't bring your family, you'll need to arrange child care. Obviously, travel writing also involves traveling, so you'll be away from your home, family, and day-to-day business responsibilities.

Compensation: Travel and expenses are usually paid to get you on location.

Event hostess: New York City is a hotbed for these types of opportunities. Many times a brand or company will reach out to bloggers and ask them to host an event. The beauty of this is that the company is relying on your reputation and readership to fill an event with guests. This is such a great opportunity because the brand co-hosts it.

Activities and responsibilities: Inviting guests and posting about the event afterward. You sometimes host at your own home or another agreed-upon location.

Pros: Parties are fun.

Cons: Planning and execution can be a lot of work.

Compensation: None.

Moms Know Best: Trying on Yes, Trying on No

To put all this opportunity knocking and decision making into practical terms, we've asked some of our tribeswomen to share their real-life stories on the subject.

Sommer Poquette, Green and Clean Mom,
http://greenandcleanmom.org/

*After you've spent three years of blogging and working with PR,
there comes a sense of loyalty to your readers, your contacts, and the
brands you've worked with and love, as well as your community.
I've been approached by competitors of companies I am very loyal
to for spokesperson opportunities, travel, brand ambassador campaigns, coupons, and free stuff. Figuring out what's good for your
family, your brand, and online relationships becomes a struggle at
times, with fuzzy lines and unclear expectations.*

*Most recently I have had to decline opportunities to be "dressed"
for conferences because the items were not sustainable, organic, fair
trade, or anything along the lines of "green." Sure, I would love new
clothes and to be decked out for a trip, but if it doesn't fit my niche
blog, what I write about, and what my community expects me to
write about, I have to say no. I also say no to personal care products
and baby care products on a daily basis. Many of them make false
claims, and when I ask questions of the PR team or the person sending the email, I cannot get answers.*

*Many companies get excited about social media and throw out the
pitch, not understanding whom they're pitching to, and then seem surprised when I say no to a cup, toy, or other product that contains toxic
ingredients. It was hard to say no, but I had to decline an opportunity to
fly to a wonderful conference because I did not agree with the company's
policy of not disclosing their ingredients. I could not write about the
company on my blog and help promote them the way they wanted to be
promoted if I did not know what was in the product. I really wanted
to attend this conference, but I have standards and cannot compromise
them for a free trip. I've also become pretty selective with trips because
leaving my family has to be worth my time, via money or future connections and advancement in my career and business.*

I also say no to books daily because I do not have time to read every book, and not every book is worth my time to review or share with my readers.

I'm not a saint, but I've certainly learned over time what fits well, what works for me, and how to be true to who I am. It's not easy, because I would love to go on fancy trips or have a new wardrobe, for example. However, I have to weigh at all times what this is worth in the long run—the products are never really "free."

Candace Lindemann, Mamanista, www.mamanista.com

We have to turn down more opportunities than we can accept. There's just not enough time to answer every single email, review every product, or go on every trip. We get about a dozen product review or trip pitches a day, plus another dozen press releases, coupon code offers, and other various email inquiries. Since we only post about one review a day, we have to be selective.

About two years ago I turned down a baby plate because, after multiple correspondences, I could not get concrete reassurance that there was no BPA in the plate. About a month later, the PR person sent a mass email asking all bloggers to scrap their reviews of the plate because the manufacturer had "discovered" that it contained BPA and that it was now a chemical of concern.

We'll also turn down an opportunity when a company tries to dictate how to run our site. We've had companies (only a few) contact us expecting that we post a certain number of times, on certain dates, include video or pictures of our families, and clear any negative feedback with them first. We're happy to accept samples for review consideration, but this is our site. If a company wants to control the message, they need to purchase an advertisement.

MIND YOUR MANNERS

If a selective opportunity or special invitation comes your way, you're going to need to respond, whether your answer is yes or no. You don't want to let much time pass. You're being judged on your speed—and if you don't want the gig, another blogger will likely be approached.

If you say yes, jump in immediately. Give 110 percent. If you're posting something on behalf of another company, send the post to the PR team that contacted you, so they know you followed through. Then send a thank-you note if you want to do more work for that team.

If you say no, it's important not to burn the bridge. The team approaching you may represent hundreds of clients, one of which you couldn't live without and would happily plug until your dying day. Also, send a thank-you note, explaining why you're not going to be able to help them out. When we say no, if it's applicable we recommend a friend or contact who might be a good fit. This is a great habit to get into, as both the PR firm and your friend will appreciate getting connected. And they'll both remember you for it!

FULL DISCLOSURE

Let's pretend you're a daily visitor to a site called waterlovers.com. You're a huge water lover, and so is the blog founder. Though it seems impossible, every day this blogger has 500 words to write about water. But one day you visit the site, and the blog author is—gasp—touting the medical benefits of drinking juice. You don't like juice, and you're pretty sure the blogger doesn't like juice either. So what's up? Has the blogger been paid to pump up XYZ brand's juice? You smell a rat. Then you notice the juice ad in the right-hand column of the blog page. The rat is just getting riper by the second. You're about to click away from the site and never return when you see the word "disclosure" at the bottom of the juice post. "Disclosure: XYZ Juice sponsored this post. As always, my opinion is not influenced by payment, and all thoughts and opinions are my own. Note: Wonder why we skipped our regularly scheduled programming today? I don't typically do sponsored content on my website, but my daughter's wisdom teeth need to be extracted, and our insurance doesn't cover that. Talking juice pays every now and then!"

The disclosure is the difference between your remaining a faithful follower of waterlovers.com and your never returning again.

Point: full disclosure is essential! Bloggers have become successful thanks to their authenticity and approachability. Real people relate to bloggers because they see just another person like themselves.

We feel that transparency is critical. If you have a relationship with a company, get a product sample for free, or travel to a destination for free, then you need to let your readers know this. If you don't, you'll lose the trust of your readers, as they might wonder if your rave review was influenced by the freebies. Also, if you're ever paid to post about a particular topic, it's still critical to share your true opinion. It's okay to give a balanced perspective, but it needs to be your own honest response, or you're going down a dangerous path.

If you don't believe us about full disclosure, believe others in our community who started an actual website called Blog with Integrity to motivate bloggers to use full disclosure. The Blog with Integrity website shares a pledge for bloggers to sign that they will indeed Blog with Integrity. You can grab a badge to display on your blog from their website: www.blogwithintegrity.com.

Here's the pledge that Susan Getgood, Liz Gumbiner, Kristen Chase, and Julie Marsh, all cofounders of Blog with Integrity, created:

Blog with Integrity

By displaying the Blog with Integrity badge or signing the pledge, I assert that the trust of my readers and the blogging community is important to me.

I treat others respectfully, attacking ideas and not people. I also welcome respectful disagreement with my own ideas.

I believe in intellectual property rights, providing links, citing sources, and crediting inspiration where appropriate.

I disclose my material relationships, policies, and business practices. My readers will know the difference between editorial, advertorial, and advertising, should I choose to have it. If I do sponsored or paid posts, they are clearly marked.

When collaborating with marketers and PR professionals, I handle myself professionally and abide by basic journalistic standards.

I always present my honest opinions to the best of my ability.

I own my words. Even if I occasionally have to eat them.

SIGNING UP FOR FREEBIES, INVITATIONS, AND CELEBRITY OPPORTUNITIES

So you're reading this chapter and thinking, "What are they talking about? I don't get pitches for free Cheerios, movie tickets, or a day at the zoo. And certainly, no one has ever approached me with a free iPhone or an invitation to go on an African safari to cover environmental degradation in Zambia. What do I have to do to get an offer like that?" Well, first things first. It may not be your moment yet. Sometimes it's just a matter of traffic, and if your numbers are low (less than 5,000 regular visitors each month, say), you may just be flying below the radar.

There's no right amount of traffic that automatically gives someone an opportunity. We have to profess that we don't have nearly the amount of traffic from daily loyal readers that some bloggers can be credited with. However, we've done a good job being savvy businesswomen, networking with the right bloggers and companies that we aspire to work with, and establishing ourselves with press coverage as go-to moms in the digital space—especially as experts in fashion and mom/children's products. There are infinite companies out there to work with. You just need to find the ones that align with your personal brand so that you can both form a mutually beneficial relationship.

Top Five Ways to Get Noticed: Approaches from Both Sides

If you think you're an up-and-coming blogger, are growing traffic and influence, and deserve a chance to say yes or no to an opportunity but simply haven't had one cross your path, here are a few ideas to consider, from the perspective of a PR professional as well as our own as bloggers:

THE PR PROFESSIONAL'S PERSPECTIVE
(courtesy of PR specialist Heather Bandura)

1. Get press for yourself—that's one of the primary ways I find new bloggers. I also also look at "As Seen In" sections of the website to see that this person is valued as a trusted resource. Also try entering independent blogger awards.

2. Get a .com (or .net, etc) URL instead of hosting your blog on Blogspot or the like. It just makes you appear more mainstream and professional. Also, spend time and money to make your site gorgeous and unique. The look and feel of a site influence my decision on whether to work with it.

3. Make it very clear on your site that you are open to working with PR people, and be clear on what you like and don't like. Provide an email.

4. Don't just focus on product reviews. For some of my clients with larger budgets, we're looking to work with bloggers on larger content campaigns. We find that there's sometimes more value in posts that provide readers with tips, recipes, advice, photos, and so on.

5. Get involved with Facebook and Twitter, and increase your fans/followers. This shows you have a fan base behind just site statistics. Clients are asking for measurement criteria.

When working with traditional press, we give circulation or viewership numbers. Social media numbers are becoming a very valued measurement tool for us, above and beyond site statistics that either aren't readily available or don't tell the whole story.

OUR PERSPECTIVE AS BLOGGERS

1. Consider reviewing a product that you haven't been asked to review and putting it under a PR person's nose (they're easy enough to find on Twitter). Make it an honest, gripping review that the company can't ignore.

2. Make sure you're not trying too hard. This might take the form of "stalking" PR people; writing overly positive reviews (such as those with too many exclamation points), or sharing useless info (such as "I ate a ham sandwich"). People know a fake when they see one. If you receive a cold shoulder from a PR person, take the hint. Either you've pushed things too far or too fast, or they're simply not interested in a private exchange.

3. Share your accomplishments. If you've just been published in a magazine or done a TV segment or gotten a great opportunity, let PR people know it. Create a press page on your site, too.

4. Try to meet the PR person face-to-face by attending a conference or other meeting that you know that person will be attending.

5. Help them out. Many times a PR person needs content to go up fast. If an opportunity like this arises, and it's a brand or cause that aligns with you, then consider posting it for them. It's a great way to help someone out and get to know the PR person better.

Some people expect that success will come overnight. It doesn't always happen that way. Trust us. Just as you're not likely to win the lottery on the first try, it's unlikely you'll land an incredible opportunity after two weeks of blogging. But you need to put yourself in position for those opportunities.

If you aspire to write reviews or become an expert in a specific area, start by writing again and again about the topics that interest you, regardless of whether a company is sending you the information. This way you will place yourself in that online space and slowly build up a reputation and credibility. Before you know it you might start getting free samples or an invite to see an advance screening of a film.

And here's a hot tip: if you want to find out which PR person reps a specific product or brand, Google to find press releases about the product or company. Usually the releases will include the PR person's email and phone number. Send them a review you've written on a product they rep, so they know you're a natural advocate for the brand.

Also, consider signing up for networks that will send you invitations to attend events or offers to sample new products. Working on a campaign is a great way to gain additional exposure. The networks below reach out to bloggers on behalf of big brands to find individuals who might participate in marketing campaigns:

Izea and Social Spark, www.izea.com

Mom Central, www.momcentral.com

Mom Select, www.momselect.com

My Blog Spark, www.myblogspark.com

One 2 One Network, www.one2onenetwork.com

Role Mommy Network, www.rolemommy.com

Social Moms, www.socialmoms.com

Clever Girls Collective, www.clevergirlscollective.com

We also want to mention here that there are bloggers who prefer to decline opportunities that come with products, compensation of any kind, and trips. We absolutely respect and understand that many bloggers just want to be diarists recording their lives or to post only topics relating directly to their niche topic. Though we accept products and compensation, we feel we should mention that there is absolutely no reason why any blogger should have to accept anything. Your blog is your platform. It's your home online. You have the ability to do with it anything you like. Again, this is the power of being a blogger. The canvas you create is your own.

And there are some opportunities that do come with no strings. But don't expect a trip to Paris to come without them! There are interviews by magazines and newspapers, invitations to conferences, and opportunities to contribute writing a major magazine or newspaper. None of these require you to wear another team's colors.

However, for most bloggers—or at least for those of you who bought this book—making money and working from home is probably your primary interest. The next step will be a deep dive into how to monetize your website, your digital brand, and your budding social media skills. We like to call it **Step 5: Manage the Benjamins.**

STEP 5

  ## Manage the Benjamins

We sorta head-faked you there. We told you that we'd get to the discussion of money in the previous chapter, but we never did. That's because so many of the opportunities on the Internet involve barter. Will write for shoes. Will vlog for invitation to Oscars. Will podcast for free trip to Spain. You get the idea.

Neither of us made any substantial income for quite a while. Audrey didn't make a penny until 2009, when she joined Lifetime Moms, their advertising network, and began to get paid for content creation on the LifetimeMoms.com website. By contrast, Colleen began earning revenue within the first few months. But that revenue came in the form of pennies at first— literally pennies, but those pennies added up, and she sought out a multitude of revenue sources right away.

We certainly never started out with a complicated business plan that said we had to hit a certain income threshold, or else. The beauty of a Digital Mom business, as we stated at the beginning, is that you define your own success. Money might not be part of that.

But if it is part of your goal, various incremental revenue streams are available to you, besides the unexpected opportunities discussed in Step 4 that may fall in your lap. We'll cover those in this chapter, and we'll suggest what to do with the money once you've got it.

As you're reading, keep these questions in mind. The answers you give will dictate how deep you want to go into this maze.

1. How much money do you need or want to make?

2. What are you willing to do for money?

3. Would you rather have more money or free time? Money or family time?

REVENUE STREAMS

The three main ways to earn money from a website or blog are advertising, affiliate marketing, and sponsored content. Here's what these terms mean and how you can start using each to earn money:

	Earning Potential	Content Integrity	Popularity	Ease of Use
Sponsored Posts	◑	○	◔	●
Ad Networks	◑	◑	●	●
Affiliate Programs	◑	●	◕	◕
Corporate Sponsorships	●	○	◕	◑

Advertising

If you've ever watched a beer commercial on TV during the Superbowl, then you know what advertising is at its most expensive and targeted. Companies are willing to pay big bucks for a consumer's attention, and advertising is how they get it. In an ideal situation, the advertisement has some relationship to the content it's running alongside. Football and beer. Football and chips. Football and headache medicine. That's targeted advertising.

With the fragmentation of modern media, we're now seeing ad dollars reaching new media, the Internet primary among them. A blog or website can now earn a small slice of the advertising pie. So many ads are floating around the Internet that you probably don't notice half of them. Some include the flashing banner ads for mortgage deals and text ads for shoe sales at Zappos that appear along the right margin of a Google search. In each case, someone is paying to place those ads. They might be paying Google or Yahoo! or any of the other huge websites out there, or they may be paying you, with your dedicated audience of 500, or 1,000, or 10,000 monthly visitors, all obsessed with scrapbooking, pearls, or the debate about the safety of childhood vaccines.

How to get started

But how does an advertiser find you if you're a mom working at home in her pajamas in the suburbs of Atlanta or on a farm in Iowa? The web has an answer for everything. Here is the answer: ad networks. Basically, these networks (see the box, page 129) act as middlemen, linking those who need to place strategic ads with those who have strategic places to put them. Money flows from the advertiser through the middleman (who takes a cut) to you, the Digital Mom with a web presence.

Now, you can cut out these advertising middlemen if you're feeling bold, and sell ad space directly to interested parties. In this way, you may hope to make more money. But in order for this to work, you'll need to be approached by an advertiser who sees your value. If you're big and/or assertive, this may very well occur. Be aware, though, that if you go this route, you'll also be playing the advertising sales administrative role yourself, collecting fees from your advertiser, maintaining quality control, trying to score advertising sales deals with big brands, and everything else the middleman would do if you hadn't cut him or her out. The biggest bonus of selling ads on your own, besides keeping 100 percent of the profits, is that these advertisements are often sold at a premium price, in weekly, monthly or quarterly increments that you and the advertiser agree on. This system can be a gravy train if all the parties are aboveboard and organized.

KEY ONLINE ADVERTISING DEFINITIONS

CPC: The cost per click; this means that you'll earn revenue each time someone clicks your ads. Remember, do not click your own ads! Google will penalize you for this behavior, and you'll be kicked out of their advertising AdSense program. Really, we know people to whom this has happened.

CPM: The cost per thousand impressions; this means that for every 1,000 page views your banner ad receives, you'll receive the dollar value earned. Average CPMs range from $2 to $4, while the more lucrative ad networks earn their partners upward of $5 to $8 per 1,000 page views, if not far more.

CTR: The click-through rate is a way to measure the success of advertising campaigns. It is calculated by dividing the number of users who click on an ad by the number of times an ad was served up to view.

Interactive Advertising Bureau (IAB) ad unit sizes: The standard sizes generally accepted on the web. You'll want your website design or layout to accommodate them:

- 728 × 90: The large leaderboard-style ads you see at the top or bottom of a web page.

- 160 × 600: The skyscraper-style ads you often see on the right-hand column of a web page.

- 300 × 250: The large rectangular ads you often see on the right-hand column of a web page.

- 125 × 125 or 150 × 150: The button ads that are especially popular with small businesses looking to reach your unique blog audience.

- Impressions: Each individual view of your website.

Page views: How many cumulative pages are viewed on your website over a period of time. The higher the page views, the longer people are staying at your site and the more likely your readers are truly engaged with your content.

Unique visitors: The number of unique people visiting your site on a daily, weekly, or monthly basis. If the same person comes three times in one day, that is still only one unique visitor.

Working with advertising networks

The big gorilla of ad networks is Google. Ads, after all, are what make Google the multibillion-dollar company it is today—hence the private jets, the landing strips, and the sense that Google is taking over the world. The beauty of GoogleAds is that everyone is welcome to participate, from the baby-blog with two visitors a month to the megasite with millions passing through. This makes Google a very egalitarian middleman. And you, as founder of your site, decide where to place the Google text links or banner ads (other middlemen aren't always so friendly). Also, with Google's text link ads you are paid when a reader clicks through the ad. So depending on your click-through rate, you can make more or less money, which is different for everyone depending on how well Google performs for them.

You can also add these Google text links to your RSS feed. In case we just lost you there, RSS is short for Really Simple Syndication, and readers use these feeds to follow frequently updated blogs or websites. In other words, if readers subscribe to their favorite blogs' RSS feeds, the updated content appears in an aggregrator website where they can either read just the title and a short excerpt from the post, or click through to the website to read even more.

Mercedes Levy, from Common Sense with Money (www.common sensewithmoney.com), blogs daily about free samples, the latest coupons on groceries, and deals at major food stores. But once she added Google ads to her RSS feed, she doubled her revenue. In her words, "After I added AdSense to my feeds in March 2009, my revenue from AdSense went from $400 a month to $966 the following month. These days my CPM with AdSense ranges from $3 to $6. To me that has translated to as much as $4,450 a month." If you wonder why this move doubled her Google AdSense revenue, the simple answer is that many readers had been missing her ads because they subscribed to her blog and read it only via their email or a reader, rather than by traveling to her site. By adding these AdSense ads to her RSS feed, all these subscribers now saw them and had the opportunity to click on them.

You might also be asking if specific ads are selected for your site. Google's algorithms determine what ads appear on any given website at any given time based on the content on the web page. If you have rich content, the ads offered up will align well with it. For Colleen, each product review on Classy Mommy means ads for the same or related products—ads that are usually of interest to her readers. When readers click through these ads, she makes money. It might be as low as only $.07 per click, but it all adds up!

The higher your traffic numbers, the more likely people will click on your Google ads. That's just Probability 101. Likewise, the more specific your content, the more specific the Google ads will be, making it more likely your traffic is lured to click them. (By contrast, diarist bloggers often tell us that their Google ads are less successful because their content is different from day to day.)

KEY NETWORKS TO KNOW

While these are the ad networks we hear the most about in the Digital Mom space, many other niche networks may be relevant to you and your blog depending on the content you create, from sports to food to beauty.

BlogHer: www.blogher.com
Federated Media: www.federatedmedia.net
Lifetime: www.lifetimemoms.com
Glam: www.glam.com
Real Girls Media: www.realgirlsmedia.com
Blog Ads: www.blogads.com
Martha's Circle: www.marthascircle.com
Food Buzz Network: www.foodbuzz.com
Natural Path Media: www.naturalpathmedia.com
Simple Earth Media: http://simpleearthmedia.com
Important Media: http://importantmedia.org

You should note that these ad networks will keep a percentage of your revenue. The amount they keep can vary, and you can sometimes negotiate what that percentage will be. Generally, a 50/50 split dominates the landscape, but we've heard that some bloggers keep between 70 and 80 percent of revenue and others keep only 40 percent of revenue.

YouTube content advertising

Yes, you can earn revenue from the YouTube videos you create. However, placing ads on any one video is by invitation only, and the particulars on YouTube's advertising program are difficult to find. If you are invited to participate, YouTube will generally place a text link ad below your video. If someone clicks on that ad, you'll earn revenue per click and be paid on a CPM basis, too. We've both been invited into the YouTube content advertising program on a per-video basis only a handful of times. The videos we've been asked to participate with are those that perform very well quickly, or that over time have received views in the 15,000-plus range. Some individuals make a ton of money on YouTube and are invited into an even more exclusive advertising program that looks to be very lucrative. Their videos become even more popular as YouTube features them, which consequently earns the vlogger even more revenue. However, YouTube keeps this info about this exclusive program confidential, and their guidelines on how one gets invited are not available to mere mortals like ourselves.

Still, our limited success pays, and it might pay for you, too. In general, we both make about $50 per month from our YouTube content advertising, but one month Colleen had a big hit with a Huggies video and made over $500 in a few weeks. Audrey had a big hit with a "What to Wear with Leggings" video. The trick is to figure out what works for you. How you title a video and what category you put it in definitely matter. Also, the more subscribers you get, the more views you'll get, and the more likely you will be invited to place ads on your videos.

Here's the link to YouTube's Partner Program: www.youtube.com/partners.

Affiliate Marketing

Affiliate marketing rewards a website—like momgenerations—when it refers readers to a location where a purchase or sales lead transaction can be made. The key to affiliate marketing for a Digital Mom is making sure that the product you're pushing and being rewarded for is interesting to your readers.

If it isn't, not only will you receive no rewards (because your readers won't be tempted to buy what you're writing about), but your readers will be annoyed that you even mentioned this product.

Commissions are usually small, ranging from 4 to 15 percent (of the sale that your link led to) with 8 percent being the average that Classy Mommy sees in her own business. But if your traffic is large, those little bits can add up. And even if your traffic is not all that high, but you have loyal readers who listen to your advice and might love the products you're aligned with, they may end up making a purchase.

The easiest affiliate marketing program to join is Amazon. (Go to amazon.com for more info on their program.) Their links are ultra-easy to implement. Plus, they pretty much sell every product on the planet, so at some point in time you could use an affiliate link organically in your content when you refer to a book you are reading or the new blender you're obsessing over to make fruit smoothies for breakfast.

For Colleen, eBay has been a small windfall. She refers her readers to eBay for every product she features on her website, giving them an option to shop for it on eBay for less. This one move increased her revenue every month with no further work required. (Go to www.ebaypartnernetwork.com for more details on their program.) Although she wishes she could tell you it made her $10,000 a month, that's not the case. However, as a blogger you need to think about all possible revenue streams. She now earns about $200 to $500 per month from her eBay affiliate program, depending on the month.

Most retailers that sell products online have an affiliate marketing program you can join. Look for it on their homepage, and then sign up with all your information and hope to be accepted. The criteria for selection for affiliate programs depend on each specific retailer. Generally, retailers are looking for websites that also have similar content. In other words, stores like The Gap or Macy's would like fashion or lifestyle bloggers, so a political blogger would not be a good fit. Sign-ups are simple and usually require you to provide a description of our website and your estimated monthly traffic, including number of page views and number of unique visitors. You can easily find these numbers from Google Analytics, the free web tool you can install on your own blog that will let you view your metrics. We advise you to add this easy-to-use tool to your blog so you can easily access your blog's statistics—and learn from them, too!

KEY AFFILIATE MARKETING PROGRAMS

ShareaSale
Amazon
eBay
Commission Junction
Pepperjam Network
LinkShare
Logical Media
My Savings Media

Moms Know Best: Monetize Gradually and Try Everything

Mindi Cherry is the owner of Moms Need to Know and Moms Need to Cook. Her sites have been the subject of several segments on the Philadelphia ABC and CBS stations.

Q: You've been successful at monetizing a blog by talking about coupons and deals. How did you do it?

A: Monetizing a blog about coupons and deals is probably much easier than monetizing other types of blogs. Readers come to my site looking for ways to save money on groceries, toiletries, household items, and clothing. All three major online coupon providers, as well as most online shopping sites, have affiliate programs, and my readers will naturally click on the links to print the coupons or take advantage of a great deal. By providing new content at a rate of seven to fifteen posts per day, I attract my readers to visit several times each day to see the newest deal—and that provides extra page views for CPM ads.

Q: Which affiliate marketing programs have worked for you? And why?

A: By signing up with several affiliate networks, I am able to offer an amazing variety to my readers. Some networks are specific to my niche, such as networks that offer mainly freebies and trial offers, but networks such as Commission Junction and Google Affiliate Network provide access to major retailers such as The Gap, Target, Macy's, and even Sephora. Because the vendors are in the networks, I don't need to reach a minimum amount with each retailer in order to get paid, and therefore I don't feel compelled to overpromote a specific retailer. Most networks have several hundred different retailers, which allows me to offer my readers deals on everything from clothing to toys to household items to books and even organic grocery items.

Q: Does one specific affiliate marketing program perform the best for you? Why?

A: Commission Junction continues to be my best performing network ten out of twelve months each year, with Amazon.com being the best at Christmas. Commission Junction provides access to popular online shopping sites such as The Gap, Old Navy, 6pm.com, and the Disney Store, as well as several photo and coupon websites.

Q: What advice for other bloggers do you have about integrating affiliate marketing content to help them monetize their blogs?

A: Integrating affiliate content has to be gradual and natural. My readers expect me to post the absolutely best deals I can find, and that is what I do, regardless of the commission I can make. While I do make an effort to post mostly the deals from vendors for which I am an affiliate, I also include plenty of deals on which I will never make a penny. People come to my site looking to save as much money as possible, and they would be annoyed if I posted a 10 percent sale at Banana Republic when a 75 percent off UGGs or Crocs is available. Those are the deals they want. Concentrate on the quality of the sale. Include any personal thoughts you may have on the product, good *or* bad. There is nothing wrong with saying "You will never catch me with a pair of Crocs Mary Janes on my feet, but I know this puts me in the minority, so here is a great sale on them!"

Q: What other practical advice do you have beyond affiliate marketing for moms to help them monetize their websites?

A: Don't forget about Google AdSense, and play with the placement of your ads to see where they perform the best. At one time, I had my Google ads fairly low on my site and was making next to nothing. By moving my ads higher on the page, I started to get better ads in those spaces and literally tripled my income from Google ads in one month. If your traffic will support it, consider selling ad space, either to small companies or to other bloggers.

Last, don't overdo it! If you are a lifestyle blogger, suddenly switching to affiliate ads in each post is going to annoy your readers and drive them away. If you are a food blogger looking to monetize, you theoretically could include a link for most of the ingredients in any given recipe, but it will quickly become obvious to your readers that you now care more about selling food and kitchen products than talking about them.

Sponsored content

Sponsored content is essentially a pay-to-post arrangement between a blogger and a company with a product or service that needs exposure. It typically takes two forms:

1. A specific message sent from a company that is to be shared with your readers. You post it; you get paid.

2. A prompt to write about a topic. You write about it in whatever form or style you wish, and then attribute the post to the company that requested it. For instance, Colleen once wrote a post about her "Wired Life" and how technology influenced her day-to-day interactions with her kids, husband, family, and friends. At the end of the post, she included a disclosure that this post was sponsored by Best Buy. That was it. Colleen didn't even mention Best Buy in the body of the post. Audrey writes fashion and beauty posts every day on her blog, but she is able to use her life (as a busy mom of four) as the main angle in the post. She doesn't drill the particular brand of makeup, shoes, or clothing over and over again. She naturally writes about her life and then adds in the particular sponsored content. Our main advice: just make sure the content you're writing works in your life and is a natural fit.

Of all the monetizing possibilities for Digital Moms, sponsored content is probably the most controversial. But we feel that if it's done with content that fits your blog and serves your readers, you don't need to apologize for it.

As with banner ads, you can sell sponsored content on your own, or companies may come directly to you asking for it, making it all the more lucrative. But most of us begin with the middlemen networks: companies that link Digital Moms to companies that need "word-of-mom" marketing.

COMPANIES THAT CONNECT BLOGGERS TO BRANDS

Clever Girls Collective

Izea and Social Spark (pay per post)

Mom Central

Mom Select

My Blog Spark (a program with General Mills)

> One 2 One Network
> Role Mommy Network
>
> As we said in the previous chapter—and it bears repeating—when you're paid to write sponsored content on your website, or even if you've received a free sample, you must disclose this to your readers. Here's the website for the endorsement guidelines from the FTC: www.ftc.gov/bcp/edu/pubs/business/adv/bus71.shtm.

OTHER OPTIONS TO EARN REVENUE

Many other revenue avenues exist besides advertising, affiliate marketing, and sponsored content. Some of the most profitable may be the accidental consulting business that grows out of your areas of expertise. Opportunities also abound for the brand and social media presence you create for yourself online. Most Digital Moms won't earn a salary from advertising alone but instead will scrape together all kinds of creative revenue streams. Here's a rundown on all the indirect ways you may earn money as a result of hanging your digital shingle.

THE DIGITAL MOM CLASSIFIEDS

Freelance writing gigs: Because of the success of our blogs, we were both invited to write for LifetimeMoms.com, part of the Lifetime television network. Colleen writes about products, Audrey writes about fashion, and we both receive a monthy paycheck for our posts on that site. But online magazines aren't the only places that need freelance writers. Brands will often launch microsites or blogs and hire Digital Moms to write some or all of the content for those sites. We've both done posts for Clorox, Pampers, Wisk, Huggies, and other brands, creating feature articles and sometimes even videos for company websites.

Activities and responsibilities: Writing an article for another company that hires you to create content for their website or blog. You might report on an event you attend on their behalf, like a movie premiere, or you might simply contribute a post on your experiences as a parent.

Pros: Writing for another website is a great way to build your résumé, introduce your writing and online persona to other readers, and potentially earn a regular paycheck.

Cons: You'll have deadlines to meet, and you'll be creating content for another source besides your own blog.

Compensation: A low of $10 per post to an average high of $250 to $500 per post when you work with a big brand.

Moms Know Best: On Getting Hired for a Writing Gig

Linsey Knerl lives on a small Nebraska farm with her business partner husband and five rambunctious kids. Her freelance writing career highlights include *PC Magazine*, *Forbes*, and AOL, and her work-at-home tips can be found on her website: www.1099mom.com. Here's one of our favorite pieces of advice:

Get a toe in one door, then use your elbow to open another. One of my best clients right now is AOL. I knew they were a tough company to get into, but I saw an article about how they were using freelancers now more than ever. When their new Seed site, www.seed.com, opened up, I felt that my chances of having an article published against thousands of others were slim, but when an open call for parenting writers went out, I knew I was more than qualified! This helped me out later when they were looking for political writers. While I hadn't done this kind of writing before, I knew that I was qualified, and it was something I really wanted to do, so I applied. Because I already had that relationship with the company for writing about parenting, they gave me a shot, and now I write for many of their sites, including food, gardening, fashion, and more! The moral of the story is to get your foot in the door with what you're known to be good at, then don't be afraid to push it open a little more every so often with new niches you'd like to explore. You have room to grow (and even make a few errors) if you've already developed a good rapport with a company or their editors.

Twitter party hostess: With the infinite number of companies trying to connect to moms online via social media channels, Twitter has exploded as a place for instant access and connections between brands and the everyday individual. As you get to know PR firms or brands and build your own online social media presence, you might be asked to host a Twitter party for a specific brand or company—and be paid to do so.

Activities and responsibilities: Twitter parties typically last from sixty to ninety minutes, and as a host you'll be responsible for asking questions and engaging the audience. You'll talk about the product or brand that is sponsoring the party, and create content that relates to the brand in some way. For instance, for the Healthy Choice Twitter party that we hosted, we had a series of conversation starters that had to do with leading a healthy lifestyle. ("When do moms find time to exercise?" or "How do moms get kids to eat their veggies?") Then we sprinkled in some questions that led to a discussion of our favorite Healthy Choice meals as well as nutritional info.

Pros: Short time commitment to host, usually only sixty to ninety minutes. You can gain new followers, as people want to follow the hosts of the party to participate.

Cons: Most successful Twitter parties take place in the evening, so it might cut into dinnertime or your child's bedtime routine, depending on your family's schedule. Your followers may get annoyed with your "commercial" tweeting during the one or two hours of your Twitter Party. You might even lose some followers. We caution bloggers to host these parties only when they pay well and feature brands that fit you.

Compensation: $500 to $1,500 for the average Mom Blogger to host. Super-duper influentials and consulting firms charge much more for this service, sometimes as much as $5000. Our tips: definitely don't do this one for free, and don't forget to send your invoice to the company!

Brand ambassador: Brands want to align with influential moms who are passionate and knowledgeable about brand-specific products and topics that relate to that brand's mission. A group of moms or an individual mom is often chosen to serve the role of brand ambassador.

Activities and responsibilities: Write blog posts, tweets, or Facebook status updates that let you share your passion for, and knowledge of, the brand. For instance, Audrey and Colleen, known as undomestic divas who are devout microwave chefs, did a compensated campaign for Healthy Choice that involved blog posts about our struggles to get our children to eat vegetables.

Pros: Great résumé builder, and aligns your blog or business with a brand. It's an excellent way to build strong relationships with the PR team or brand managers.

Cons: Be careful that you don't turn yourself or your blog into a commercial.

Compensation: We're seeing a high of about $250 per blog post, up to $500 for video posts; some opportunities come in at $25 per post or less.

Social media consultant: This could be a one-time project that will take four hours or a long-term gig that calls for you to consult for twenty hours a month for a year. You create the terms with the firm and earn either a project fee or an hourly fee. You can advise on their strategy for blogger, Twitter, YouTube, or Facebook outreach.

Activities and responsibilities: Blogger outreach, developing social media strategies, sharing best practices across the industry.

Pros: Lets you utilize your professional skills in a flexible way—often from home and on an hourly or project basis. Great résumé builder, and good for networking, too.

Cons: Not a regular paycheck unless you sign a long-term agreement. You might need to leverage your own personal network of bloggers if you are handling an outreach campaign. You might annoy your friends if the offer is to review a not-so-hot product for "free" while you are earning the consulting dollars.

Compensation: Hourly or by project.

Social media community manager: Sometimes a company becomes so impressed by your social media savvy that you're hired part-time or full-time to manage the company's social media strategy or to act as their company voice on their social media platforms. Contracts can be hourly or monthly or even for a chunk of hours per day, as they might need you to handle their message boards, Twitter handle, or Facebook page (like 12 to 4 p.m. or 8 to 12 p.m.).

Activities and responsibilities: You will be expected to live on Twitter and/or Facebook on behalf of the company, helping spread their marketing message.

Pros: A regular paycheck, high visibility, résumé builder.

Cons: Regular time commitment—time that is spent growing or supporting another company instead of putting your efforts into growing your own business.

Compensation: Agreed-upon hourly rates, or salary.

Blogger correspondent: Today, instead of relying only on the media to cover events, companies will sometimes hire moms to be correspondents. What do we offer? Real mom perspective. Audrey was hired by Quaker Oats to interview Miranda Cosgrove, the star of *iCarly*, shadowing her around for an entire day to promote their after-school playground initiative. Companies will want you to tweet and Facebook live, along with shooting video and posting when you can, on location. Later, you can write a post or upload your video to your own website; the brand can also use the content for their own purposes according to the contract you sign.

Activities and responsibilities: Serve as a correspondent from the red carpet at the People's Choice Awards for Tide, shadow Miranda Cosgrove (*iCarly*) for Quaker Chewy, attend the Oscars for Kodak.

Pros: These are typically one- to two-day jobs with high visibility. The pay is typically excellent, and the events you cover are often once-in-a-lifetime experiences. Being a blogger correspondent truly gives you unique access and amazing material for your blog.

Cons: Child care may be interrupted, the reporting is hard work, and you'll most likely need to travel to cover the event.

Compensation: Travel and expenses are covered. Day rates average about $1,500.

Company spokesperson: An opportunity to speak on behalf of a company at an event or via any media outlet, from vlogging to talking on TV.

Activities and responsibilities: Here are some samples of what we've done: an eight-week spokesperson contract with Mattel, including the production of two blog posts, two TV segments (national and local), and one radio spot; an eight-week contract with T.J.Maxx/Marshall's Back-to-School, including hosting Twitter parties, twenty-four tweets, Facebook updates, six blog posts, and up to ten TV interviews, and a trip to LA to cover the Teen Choice celebrity gifting suite to promote T.J.Maxx's totes that benefit and raise funds for Save the Children; a one-year contract with Scrubbing Bubbles to do radio and print interviews, host a blogger event, and post about the brand on our social media platforms.

Pros: Always paid; could be for one month to one year, depending on your contract. Great exposure for your personal brand, and a huge résumé builder that might help you get hired for future well-paid spokesperson gigs.

Cons: Hard work with lots of hidden jobs (like having to dress up extras in the TV segments) and lots of zigzag travel all over the country, which can wreak havoc on your home life.

Compensation: $5,000 to $100,000 depending on the term of your agreement, the noncompeting contract you sign, and the amount of activities you are tasked with during the term.

Twitter advertising: If you've got a lot of followers, companies can pay you to send out sponsored tweets from your own Twitter handle. This is known as instream advertising. Typically, after you sign up for a Twitter advertising program, your tweets will be priced based on the number of followers you have. When you get an offer to send out a specific tweet, you can decline or accept. The companies we both are familiar with include ad.ly and Sponsored Tweet.

Pro: This is one more revenue source to add to your income, and it takes just about zero work to send out a tweet. (They even usually write it for you!)

Cons: You'll perhaps annoy your followers if you send too many ads or if the ads are not relevant to your area of expertise.

Compensation: The average price range is based on your number of followers. For instance, Colleen earns about $11 per tweet, while Audrey earns closer to $18 because she has more followers.

Moms Know Best: Get Creative and Be a Resource for Others

Laurie Turk, www.TipJunkie.com

I love the quote "Poverty breeds ingenuity." It's so true! After having unexpected back surgery, all of a sudden I found myself with $12,000 in medical debt. The economy was terrible and everyone was struggling, so handmade businesses by bloggers were on the rise. Therefore, I co-created a text ad widget for women with small online

> *businesses. We kept the Visit Our Peeps widget (www.chicchickme-dia.com/peeps) really affordable, only $5.95 a month. Within two months we had sold three hundred text ads! Thanks to the influential blogging friends who endorsed the widget, we earned $20,000 in twelve months! It was a wonderful blessing to be able to pay off that medical debt while helping fellow women in business in a very inexpensive way.*

SELLING YOURSELF

Now you know all the different ways to make money, but will you get out there and hustle for them? This is not a passive process. Getting an ad network or affiliate or direct advertiser often requires pitching yourself—your ideas, intellect, creativity, and work ethic. When you're working with a brand that has an annual budget of $30 million for marketing and advertising, don't feel bad telling them you deserve to be paid. We know many moms who have made that mistake, and sadly, some companies just go along with it. The tides seem to be turning, and more and more moms are getting paid for their work. Still, don't let yourself be taken advantage of. Ever.

Create a Media Kit

One of the first steps toward proving your worth is creating a media kit. You'll use this kit to share everything about you and your site. This is your chance to shine, show your professionalism, and play hardball. Everyone from local mom-owned shops selling handmade burp cloths to potentially interested brands like Tide, Target, or Coca-Cola will see this document. Here's the info to include:

Your bio

Your website's history and focus

Stats about your website (unique visitors monthly, monthly pageviews)

Ad sizes offered

Pricing per ad

Other options and fees (e.g., newsletter, sponsored post, speaker fee, giveaways)

Statistics such as Alexa rank, Technorati rank, RSS subscribers, Google Page rank, number of Twitter followers, number of Facebook fans, Klout ranking

Accolades or awards you or your blog have earned

Press page (if you have created a press page on your website listing all the mainstream buzz you or your blog have received, be sure to include this document or a link to it in your media kit)

Wondering how to price your ads? Unfortunately, there is no magic answer, but here are a few strategies:

1. Offer a price that's higher than you think the advertiser is willing to pay; that gives you room to negotiate.

2. Try to secure a high ad price by bundling it with some other incentives, like hosting a giveaway.

3. Try to secure a high ad price, but promise a discount for long-term ad buys. This guarantees you'll sell more ad space for a longer time, and again gives you room to negotiate.

4. Find a network of bloggers, or others in the industry whom you trust, and talk over their monetizing practices. You will be surprised by the range of strategies.

Pitch Yourself

With the media kit in hand, it's time to pitch. Pitch what? Yourself, your website, your tribe, and your creative ideas. Yes, these well-paid teams of marketers and PR professionals need your ideas. And if you can't come up with great ideas, they will turn to the next blogger in their Rolodex. They need to know how your blog or vlog or podcast is going to help them sell their brand, service, or product. They want new, fresh, and catchy. A video contest. A free giveaway with hidden grand prize winners. A vlog wrapped in a podcast, topped with a choreographed dance. Seriously, though, pitching ideas is the best part of the sell—and also the most precarious. Offer enough imaginative ideas to engage the company reps, so they can envision the campaign. Remember, they are busy people juggling many accounts and budgets. Inventing a campaign with you isn't their top priority unless you make it their top priority. Just be sure not to share all of your brilliant ideas before a contract is signed!

Moms Know Best: Pitching Without Pitching It Away

Julie Pron is the owner and editor of Just-Precious.com and the Bloggers' Book Club. In the spring of 2010, she cofounded Just Centsible Consulting with her business partner, Kelly Whalen. Julie has served as a Staples Holiday Blogger and a Bravado Mama Ambassador, and she currently acts as a panelist for the planning of an upcoming daytime talk show.

Q: **How did you pitch your new consulting company to get clients?**

A: It's most important to identify a company's needs. Find an area that they are lacking, brainstorm an idea that will benefit them, and pitch that. Make sure you pitch a brief outline of an idea. Don't give away the farm, so to speak.

Q: **As a consultant, you both learned the hard way that securing a contract early in a relationship is critical. Why?**

A: When we first started out, Just Centsible was approached

by a Fortune 500 company. As requested, we pitched an idea to them. We gave that company every last detail of a huge campaign. And we way underquoted them because this was our foot in the door. After about three weeks of back-and-forth with the company and hours of conference calls with our "client," we realized that they were asking and asking—asking but not paying. And the contract we negotiated still hadn't been signed.

It was hard to do, but Kelly and I had to put our foot down. We finally told our "clients" that we could do no more conference calls with them until we had a signed con-tract. They continued to request calls with us, asking more and more questions. But we recognized that opening our mouths to give more wouldn't help us. We needed to get something in return to pay for our ideas and our feedback. Finally, when we told them we wouldn't take their calls again until we received a signed contract, they told us it would be signed within a week. Two weeks later, we received an email saying that they had opted to go with a different PR firm that wasn't charging for the program. They asked us if we would still work with them as members of the campaign. When we responded that it wouldn't be appropriate, they told us,"It's a shame; we feel we'll be missing a lot of great concepts and ideas by not working with you." Yes, indeed, they would!

I still haven't decided what is most infuriating—that this Fortune 500 company stole our ideas and contracted with another PR company to run the exact same campaign that we wrote, that a "PR company" is doing all of this work for free (thereby hurting the social media community by giving away their ideas and time for nothing, while the rest of us watch our worth go to nothing), or that we spent hours and hours for very little respect.

But I did learn a few things in the experience:

1. Never give more than a summary in a pitch.

2. Never use your brainpower without compensation.

3. Never work with a company that doesn't respect the people they claim to work with.

I used this experience to help myself grow. I have worked with more than one Fortune 500 company now, but when this was the only one, even without a contract, it was on my résumé as having worked with them. The company may never have made it to client level, but I certainly know how to work with them.

Q: What advice do you have for others starting a business, given the lessons you've learned?

A: Have a simple template and stick to it. If you're like me and write in detail, that's fine. Everything I do is in bullets to the nth degree. But when it's time to propose your idea, go to the outermost, least detailed concepts and summarize. Give your potential clients a little bite of you, but make them hungry for more. And don't accept "We don't have money for that." Any company that wants to make it in the world realizes that you have to spend something to make something. Make yourself desirable, and be that something they need to spend their money on.

INVOICING

Blah blah blah. You mean I actually have to invoice clients? Yep, you'll probably need to do this. These companies need it for their records and to trigger payment. If it's only $50 and an exchange between you and a small firm, they might just PayPal you. But if you work with a big brand, a PR firm or even another small business, chances are you will need to send an invoice and fill out a W9.

Colleen and Audrey's Tips: A Master Class in Monetizing

1. Be prepared to have advertising rates or a media kit.

2. If you are asked to provide a media kit or rates, do so quickly.

3. Remember, these big brands have gigantic marketing budgets. We're talking millions of dollars. So if the PR firm or advertising agency for a consumer packaged goods company (think razors, cereal, snacks, cosmetics, soaps, or all those goodies you buy at the grocery store or drugstore) tells you there is no budget, remember that a budget does exist. There just might not be an allocation for a digital spend on social media or to pay you. So don't feel bad saying no to a campaign if you feel you should be compensated, but the campaign budget doesn't include your work.

4. Ask for money when none is offered and you think it should be. We understand that this can be hard to do. That's why movie stars and NFL athletes have agents—so someone else can do the negotiating for them. Unfortunately, we don't have agents working for us, so we do our own negotiations. Also, if you're a mom trying to on-ramp back into your career, you are eager to take opportunities as a résumé builder.

A nice way we've found of handling the "no money" response is to email back inquiring about their offer as though compensation is involved—even though the email might have been pretty clear it was not included. Say, "Yes, I am interested. I'd love to hear more details—including the specifics on timelines, tasks, and compensation. Thanks for thinking of me for this project."

5. Be willing to walk away if you find you will not be paid or if the amount will not be fair. Like any good negotiator, know what your

walk-away point is before the negotiation begins. This way you w
feel good about your decision whatever the outcome.

6. Add those Amazon affiliate links here and there when you do
    mention your favorite book or a product you love. It may not
    seem like a lot of money, but every penny adds up. Besides, this
    will allow you to experiment and see what strategies or products
    do result in click-through sales for you. Moms work hard to save
    money and clip coupons. Likewise, make some of those same
    little efforts to make money on your blog by testing out new rev-
    enue-earning options.

7. When creating a pitch on your own for a company, or in re-
    sponse to their inquiries, share your creative ideas with them.
    They are looking for interesting ways to use Digital Moms. If you
    map out innovative ideas on how you can work together, it will
    be harder for them to pass up the opportunity of working with
    you—and you just made their job easier!

When considering pricing, we always offer a menu of three campaigns to choose from: one priced low as a bare-bones campaign,
a medium-sized campaign that includes all the bare-bones options plus a little bit more, and a big option with all the ingredients at the highest price point. This makes it easier for a company
to share the range of ideas with the key decision makers—often
PR teams, ad agencies, and the brand managers from the corporation—and show how they can work with you at different price
points.

TAX AND LEGAL CONSIDERATIONS

We don't want to bore you with legalese, so we'll be short and to the point. Once
you start earning money from your site, there are tax and legal implications.

You may decide to form an LLC (limited liability corporation) in order

ts of your family from that of your new business. You can
ne if you're feeling bold; it takes about an hour and costs
n did this for her business using the services available at
Bizfilings.com. You will want to review any and all FTC laws regarding disclosures; and you will want to study up on how your taxes will be affected by all the 1099s you'll likely collect as your company grows.

"I'm always so nervous about doing something wrong," says Julie Pron of JustPrecious. "From deciding if you'd rather form an LLC or a partnership to determining how to open a bank account, all the business stuff can be overwhelming. I have a more creative mind; I'm not much of a business-by-the-numbers type, so I get stuck on all of the legal stuff and often ignore it. It became a consistent argument for my husband and me, and I finally gave in and hired a lawyer so it wouldn't be as much of an issue for us."

We—and many bloggers we know—have consulted lawyers and accountants on these matters. Yes, they can be expensive, so you may wait until you've got enough money coming in to merit the expense. You could also seek out advice at a discount from family or friends who are lawyers; that's exactly what Audrey did. Or perhaps you can barter for legal advice (legal advice in exchange for an ad?).

If you can't hire a lawyer and/or an accountant right away, take a few free precautions, at least. At www.freeprivacypolicy.com you will find a basic privacy policy to post on your site. It tells individuals who sign up for your newsletters or leave comments how you will collect their information and how it will be used. Here too is a free disclosure policy: disclosurepolicy.org. Post this statement or a similar statement on your site if you intend to accept any money or swag in exchange for a blog posting. For more on the FTC's rules about disclosure, visit www.ftc.gov/bcp/edu/pubs/business/adv/bus71.shtm.

A Final Note on Disclosure

Remember, there are also legal reasons for disclosure. We talked to Stacy DeBroff, founder and CEO of Mom Central Consulting (www.MomCentralConsulting.com), who also has a law degree. She has been quoted or seen in *USA Today*, the *New York Times*, and the *Wall Street Journal* and has appeared on TV shows from the *Today* show to CNN.

Q: So, why, besides the loyalty of regular readers, is it important to disclose relationships with companies?

A: Last year, the Federal Trade Commission updated its guidelines to require bloggers to disclose any products or services given in exchange for a blog post. In addition to complying with FTC guidelines, bloggers who disclose these relationships ensure that their blogs are fully transparent to readers. We recommend proactive disclosures at the bottom of all posts, product reviews, or any other sponsored content appearing on a blog. The disclosure should mention that the blogger wrote a post/review while participating in a campaign on behalf of (name specific brand) and that the blogger received (identify product/incentive) to facilitate her review and to thank her for taking the time to participate.

TRADEMARKING

You may also need a lawyer to help you with the issue of trademarks. Yes, you might not be Coca-Cola, Target, or Ford Motor Company, but your business name is an asset that you need to protect. You've spent hours and hours—and in some cases years—building that brand name and establishing a reputation. You don't want someone to take that away and force you to start all over again. So, before you even hang your shingle we beg you to be sure that the name you select is not already trademarked. Otherwise, in eighteen months, after tons of hard work establishing yourself, you may find yourself getting an email letting you know that you must stop using your blog name because you are infringing on someone who already owns it. We've seen this happen to bloggers countless times. It's quite devastating.

Also, in case it isn't obvious, remember that rule about not plagiarizing in high school or college? It holds true here, too. Just as you want to protect your hard work and copyrighted material, be sure you don't steal that from others. Always give attribution if you're sharing someone else's content, and always link back to the contributing site. And, no, you cannot steal someone else's photos and use them as your own.

SAVING AND INVESTING

Your family's finances are your private affair, but now that you're probably earning money, perhaps for the first time in a while, you have some decisions to make. Will you plow the extra cash into your family's checking account or IRA? Will you open a separate business checking account (easier for your accountant to track your business expenditures) and spend money on your business? Will you grow your business or keep it as is? If you grow the business, how much are you willing to spend, and what do you need to spend money on (a new logo, a new employee, new bells and whistles on your website?).

GROWING THE BUSINESS

If you decide growing is your game, we are excited for you. But ask yourself these questions:

- What kind of growth do I seek? More profit? More readers? More consulting gigs? More size? And how much? Hundreds of dollars of growth or hundreds of millions? A few new readers or thousands?

- Do I have a business plan? (You know—the plan that predicts how your business will grow, how you should market and advertise, and exactly how many expenses you will incur? And gives grand predictions of how much money you'll someday earn from your clever idea?) Maybe you didn't make a business plan the first time around, but you might want one now that you've actually succeeded and intend to expand that success. If you don't know how to create a business plan, don't worry. Check out the following list of books for some advice about constructing a good one.

Moms Know Best: The Business Books Behind Our Businesses

These are general and informative books we found useful in our digital lives, with information ranging from marketing to entrepreneurship.

1. *The Art of the Start: The Time-Tested, Battle-Hardened Guide for Anyone Starting Anything*, by Guy Kawasaki

2. *The 10 Day MBA: A Step-by-Step Guide to Mastering the Skills Taught in America's Top Business Schools*, by Steven Silbiger

3. *The Tipping Point: How Little Things Can Make a Big Difference*, by Malcolm Gladwell

4. *Purple Cow: Transform Your Business by Being Remarkable*, by Seth Godin

5. *The 12 Secrets of Highly Creative Women*, by Gail McMeekin

6. *The Girl's Guide to Starting Your Own Business*, by Caitlin Friedman and Kimberly Yorio

7. *Getting to Yes: Negotiating Agreement Without Giving In*, by Roger Fisher, William L. Ury, and Bruce Patton

- If it's more revenue I seek, is there a way I can grow revenue without actually growing the business? (e.g., paid writing gigs, a paid freelance blogger correspondent role)

- Do I have funds to grow, or do I need a grant or small business loan?

- Can I apply for women-owned business grants to fuel my growth?

- Can I continue to manage my business alone, or do I need to hire outside contractors to help me get the job done?

- What can I do to improve my website presence? (e.g., design, logo, ad spaces)

- Can I hire a virtual assistant to help me manage my email and editorial calendar?

- Should I hire writers to contribute to my blog so I can create far more content and share a myriad of perspectives, versus continuing to be the sole contributor to my blog?

After contemplating these questions, you'll have a better idea where you need to invest your time or money to improve your business and reach your goals, whether they are growing website traffic, creating more content, or earning more revenue from seeking out unique opportunities that pay well.

Regardless of what you strive to accomplish, it's now probably time to do some homework and networking. Think Internet research, reading a few good books, and reaching out to your community of Digital Moms to ask advice. The appendix also lists some great resources with lots more information on a plethora of business-related topics. The time you spend on this homework and networking might make the difference between hiring an excellent freelance writer or blog designer, or hiring one who is a dud. Likewise, the time you spend buffing up your own media kit so you can better pitch yourself for a paid spokesperson job or writing gig might make the difference between scoring a steady salary and not getting hired.

SELLING YOUR BUSINESS

For many bloggers, the goal of spending so much time and effort growing their business is the dream of selling it for a profit. But how do you go about making that dream a reality? Here's a story of two bloggers who started with a blog post and did just that! Take a read and learn some tips in case you find yourself in this enviable position someday. It's goose-bump worthy.

Moms Know Best: The Pipe Dream

Danielle Friedland is best known as the founder and former editor in chief of the Celebrity Baby Blog, the first and largest website dedicated exclusively to celebrity pregnancies and celebrity babies, which she created in 2004 and sold to People.com in 2008. Currently working as social media and community manager for the national nonprofit Healthy Child Healthy World, and as editor of the Breastfeeding Diaries blog for Bravado Designs, she lives in Maplewood, New Jersey, with her husband and two kids, Anya, five, and Asher, one. She also volunteers as a certified lactation counselor for at-risk families. She has a Bachelor of Arts degree in criminology from Hampshire College.

Q: You're the mastermind behind Celebrity Baby Blog. What made you start it?

A: Essentially, boredom! In 2003, my husband created his food blog, thefoodsection.com, and I became a blog widow because he spent most of his free time working on it. I decided to start my own blog, so first I tried writing a personal blog called NFN Ng and then a knitting blog called D Knitty. Both were extremely boring, so I abandoned them after some time. Then, in January 2004, Josh and I were watching the Golden Globes and I was entertaining him with commentary about the nominated moms. Marcia Gay Harden was pregnant with twins, and Mary Louise Parker had just given birth to her son after Billy Crudup left her while she was eight months pregnant. He suggested that I create a new blog about the topic of pregnancy and babies in Hollywood, and I started Celebrity Baby Blog right there on my couch!

Q: How does it make you feel to see your creation on People.com? Is it surreal?

A: Whenever I feel down, I remember: Holy crap, I sold something to Time Inc., one of the largest media conglomerates in the world. It's a pinch-me kind of thing. Never in a million years would I have even guessed that the blog I started out of loneliness and boredom would have Time Inc. knocking at my door and offering me four times what they originally offered to pay for my site.

That said, I'm not fond of what People.com did to my "baby," and sometimes I wish I hadn't sold it. Then I remember that I don't have to worry about putting two kids through college, and it doesn't bother me that much.

Q: What advice do you have for someone who sells a website? What are the pros? What are the cons?

A: First thing—get an attorney experienced in mergers and acquisitions. Whatever it costs, it's worth it. Those attorneys will help you get the best deal financially but also get the terms you need. They know of things that will never occur to you. Depending on where you live, you'll pay roughly $200 to $500 an hour. (I think my deal required at least two hundred hours of my attorney's time, but we were dealing with a huge corporation, albeit on a small deal for them.) Talk to a few before hiring one. If you can, try to get one who has worked on sales of websites.

Next step is to figure out how much your site is worth. Research what other sites have sold for. If you think you have a very hot property, get it evaluated. This alone will cost around $10,000, so be fairly certain that you'll be able to sell it for many times that amount. Having that can help you, but it could also hurt you if it turns out your site is worth less than you want to sell it for.

If you want to continue working on the site, now is the time to negotiate your terms of employment. What they'll be willing to give you may range from zero to five years, but you'll want to get something in writing. Try to get a sense of whether they want you to stay on; if they do want your help transitioning, they'll be more willing to be more flexible.

Also make sure that if they want you to sign a noncompeting agreement, it doesn't preclude you from working in the field of your blog, and try to keep the length of the agreement as short as possible.

Finally, whatever you do in terms of employment, spend some time thinking about what you want out of it. I can tell you from my personal experience that it can be very difficult having a boss after operating autonomously on your site. You're used to making most, if not all, of the important decisions, and suddenly you have someone telling you how to raise this baby that you gave birth to. Imagine how you'd feel if someone started telling you how to raise your kids or care for your pet when they'd only just met you and them! It's challenging, but as long as you're prepared, it can work out.

Lindsay Ferrier writes the award-winning blended family blog Suburban Turmoil about life as a mother and stepmother to kids who are nineteen, seventeen, six, and three years old. She also writes a newspaper column based on the blog and recently started the style blog She's Still Got It, which she now writes for CafeMom, the number-one mom's site on the Internet.

Q: How long have you been blogging?

A: I started blogging in May 2005. At the time, I didn't know what a blog was—I had heard of online diaries and thought it would be fun to create my own.

Q: What have been the direction and focus of your blog? What other sites did you originally write for?

A   Soon after I started writing my blog, I discovered that my humorous posts about my life were by far the most fun to write, so I naturally headed in that direction with my stories. My first major breakthrough as a writer came after I sent the link to my blog to the editor of the *Nashville Scene* newspaper. Within an hour, she called and offered me a weekly column. At that point, I came out of the blogging closet (like most mom bloggers in 2006, I was writing under a pseudonym) and put my real name and photo on my blog. My blog traffic exploded, and the rest is history!

Q: You recently sold your very successful style blog. How long had you been writing it before you sold it? What gave you the idea to sell it?

A: I started the style blog She's Still Got It on a whim in December 2009, simply out of frustration that I couldn't find the kind of style blog that I wanted to read. I thought I'd write it for a week or two and then shut it down once readers started complaining that I didn't know what I was talking about. Instead, the opposite happened. Within a month or two, my style blog was getting the same sort of traffic that it had taken me years to build on Suburban Turmoil.

I really loved writing for She's Still Got It, and it occurred to me that if I could write my style posts for a living, I'd have the perfect job. I also knew I had the kind of intensely loyal readership that other sites desperately wanted. And so, despite the fact that everyone told me I was crazy, I decided to pitch the idea of selling the blog to a larger site and writing the posts for a salary.

Q: **How did you go about selling it? Did you pitch yourself? Please explain how you created a proposal and how you decided to pitch CafeMom rather than another online mom property?**

A: Right about the time I had the idea of selling my blog, I discovered CafeMom's blog, The Stir. The blog's off-the-cuff, no-holds-barred style was very similar to mine, and many of the writers were online friends and colleagues, so I thought it would be an excellent first place to start. I sent an email outlining my idea to Tracy Odell, senior vice president of content strategy and development for CafeMom. She asked for a proposal, and we took it from there.

Q: **Explain to our readers how this works. Did the blog totally fold into CafeMom, or does it still exist as a separate site?**

A: Because I had no interest in keeping the rights to my style posts, the transition to writing for CafeMom was seamless. I sold all of my prior content to CafeMom and now get paid to write fifteen posts per week for the site. My posts appear on The Stir's Beauty and Style channel, but readers of She's Still Got It can also link directly to my posts on The Stir as a She's Still Got It independent blog. My old site is still up, but all posts refer readers to The Stir.

Q: **What advice do you have for someone who wants to sell their blog?**

A: If you want to sell your blog, I'd recommend (in retrospect!) mapping out exactly what you want to happen and creating a proposal before you contact anyone with your idea. It's also a good idea to consult your friends and colleagues who have a gift for sealing the deal. I went to my friend Isabel Kallman (founder of Alphamom.com) for advice, and she really helped me solidify the idea in my mind and sell it to someone else.

Q: Did you ever dream this would happen to you?

A: Once I had the idea of selling She's Still Got It, it seemed like such a great deal for everyone that I couldn't imagine it not working out—I'm Pollyanna-ish that way. Now I really do have a dream job, one that I absolutely love, so I feel very, very fortunate in that respect.

Did I ever dream when I started a blog during my daughter's naptime five years ago that it would lead to this kind of success? Heck no! I still have to pinch myself all the time (figuratively, anyway!) to remind myself that this amazing experience is real.

Before we close this chapter, we just want to say that there are no sure things in business. You may start a site about windsurfing the same day as someone 1,000 miles away, and your posts may be twice as charming as theirs, and your traffic may be twice as large. But for some reason, they get all the travel junkets to Hawaii and the paid spokesperson gigs. When you're feeling jealous, sit yourself down and ask yourself if you'd be as annoyed if you didn't know about the other person's success. Would you be satisfied with your success if you weren't measuring it against someone else's, in other words? In **Step 6: Don't Forget the Children!** understanding what makes you happy and unhappy, what makes your family happy and unhappy, and ultimately what defines success for you, is key. It's key to this whole digital megillah. Without the answers, you're just running laps without a stopwatch.

STEP 6

  Don't Forget the Children!

Define Your Version of Success and Make Sure You're Truly Finding Your Middle Ground

With a laptop, smartphone, and iPad, no matter where you are, you can always be connected to your email, Facebook, Twitter, and blog—at the park, at the movies, out to dinner with friends, or even while changing a dirty diaper. We confess: there are days we're tweeting more than talking.

Every Digital Mom we know hits a moment when she must look up from her smartphone, see the crayons strewn across the floor and the crying baby across the room, and ask herself, "Am I balancing my work life with my family?" We're only human. Getting out of whack and over our heads with work is natural. Digital Moms are as vulnerable to this as the next girl, and social media can seem addictive. But we believe that a Digital Mom—because she controls her environment—can remedy the problem more easily than a mom in a corporate office setting.

So an alternative title for this step could be "Stop and Reassess," because that's what you'll have to do to get back on track. Ask yourself these questions:

How much time am I spending with my kids?

How much time do I want to spend with them?

How many hours a day am I spending plugged in?

What seems like a healthy number of hours to be plugged in?

How many hours a day am I spending on myself (not working)?

When was the last time my husband and I had dinner together?

When was the last time I got some exercise?

Am I happy?

If your answers don't please you, don't panic. You are not alone. According to Liberty Mutual's Responsibility Project, bloggers would like to spend about five and a half hours per day unplugged, but they are unplugging for an average of only four hours per day. Family time is the top reason 78 percent of bloggers like to unplug, but other motivations include hobbies and exercise.

Whatever your reasons, it's time to act. After all, your children won't always be children. As Gretchen Rubin, blogger and author of *The Happiness Project,* has said, "The days are long, but the years are short." You'll probably have to make some major adjustments as well as some minor ones. Your choice will depend on where you see yourself on the working mom spectrum.

FINDING YOUR SPOT ON THE SPECTRUM

In the introduction we talked about the middle ground and the possibility that you can find it as a Digital Mom. But you won't find it automatically just because you choose to go online. Not only can your priorities shift in good and bad ways, as described above, but some of you will find out through trial and error that you want to be more of a working mom than a nonworking mom, or vice versa. Think of it as a spectrum, with the leftmost point on the spectrum being Donna Reed (i.e., superhousewife) and the rightmost point Margaret Thatcher (full-time career woman). Where are you? Where do you want to be?

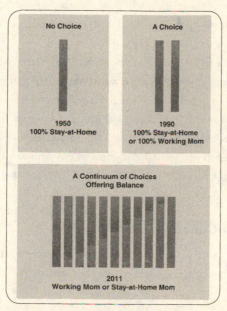

The beauty of being a digital entrepreneur is that you can change quickly in little and big ways to get yourself where you want to be. For perhaps the first time in your career, you are your own boss and have the flexibility to prioritize and choose family over work. You also get to make the executive decision to reorganize your schedule and your work calendar. Cancel a Skype call to make it to the big ballet recital. Cut Twitter out of your life entirely and make it to every dress rehearsal, band practice, and soccer game from now until eternity. Or tell your husband you're making enough money for him to quit his job, and ask him to attend every school function from now on. But you *must* choose.

Why? Because as you go deeper and deeper into Digital Mom-dom, your family, work, opportunities, and life inevitably snowball. You may have started blogging on a whim or as a hobby, not knowing what would happen, but a few months or years later you could have a full-time career. If that happens, you may very well lose sight of your original goal. Faced with new opportunities to explore, suddenly the plan to stay home with the kids and blog for intellectual stimulation while they're napping can become "I need a nanny to run the house so I can be the keynote speaker at BlogHer in New York, and nothing can stand in my way!"

How do you figure out what's right for you? You need to continually reevaluate. Where did you plan to be when you started? Where are you now? And where are you headed? How much money are you making in relation to how much you need? Why did you get into this business in the first place, and is that "why" being fulfilled now? Would you be just as satisfied with your digital career if you were making less money and spending less time at it? What is enough for you?

DEFINING SUCCESS—IT'S PERSONAL

For most of us, success is at the center of all these questions of balance. Everyone's definition of success is different, but usually it's a combination of these elements:

Money

Free time

Power

Big-ticket items (e.g., car, jewelry)

Being the mom "in the know"

Invitations to events

Maintaining a healthy lifestyle and body

Making social change

Making your children proud

Access to power and celebrity

Intellectual stimulation

Seeing your work published in print or online

Achieving lifelong goals

Becoming an expert in a specific niche or category

Time for your children

Cooking delicious dinners

A sparkling clean home

Providing comfort for your partner

And then there's the measure of your blog's success, which is a subset of your sense of success about life in general. To review, most people measure their site's success by these factors:

Monthly visitors (which you can measure with Google Analytics, www.google.com/analytics)

Twitter and Facebook followers

Comments (their abundance and tenor)

A famous blogger linking to your site

Advertising sales

Coverage in mainstream media

Invitations to speak, paid gigs, and other perks

BEWARE OF DIGITAL BURNOUT

All this updating on Twitter, Facebook, and your blog, along with an over-flowing email inbox, can get exhausting. You can feel overwhelmed, stressed out, and sometimes as if you're being pulled in a hundred different directions.

Moms Know Best: Burnout—It's Right on the Other Side of Success

Amy Lupold Bair, the founder of Resourceful Mommy, also launched a major consulting company after the wild success of her Twitter parties. She's often credited with being the inventor of the Twitter party, where brands interact with consumers who tweet to discuss products and content related to the brand as well as to win giveaways. As of the summer of 2010, she has just over 1000 members in her Global Influence Media group and has hosted three Twitter parties a week for the past year for brands like AT&T, ConAgra, and BabyCenter. This venture started on a whim and grew into a booming entrepreneurial venture.

Q: When did you realize you were in over your head?

A: I realized about a year after beginning that I would not be able to continue as I had been and still find work/life balance. I made it work by getting caught up in the evenings and weekends, but I was getting burned out doing that.

Q: What did you do to try to bring balance back to your life?

A: I made a concerted effort to be even more selective about the work I accepted, because requests for work were beginning to come in more quickly than I could fulfill. I also hired another self-employed mom to work for me on a contract-by-contract basis, relying on her sometimes on a full-time basis. Finally, I hired in-home child care for twelve hours a week for the first time in the summer of 2010, so I could devote my daylight hours to work when the kids were out of school.

Q: Did it work?

A: It did work. Knowing that you will be sitting at a computer from 1 to 5 p.m. each day allows you to enjoy the park from 9 to 11 a.m. with the kids without feeling that more than you can handle is waiting for you at home. Also, having a coworker of sorts has allowed me to go offline for the occasional vacation, which few entrepreneurs do.

Q: What's next?

A: Someday both of my children will be in elementary school full time. I raised my business and my family at the same time, and my hope is that by the time they're both in school, we'll all be hitting our stride. I realize that summers will pose a bigger challenge if the work becomes a more traditional workday, but I know now the benefit of cutting back on profit during the summer to keep both myself and my kids happy.

Q: Any other tips for moms who work from home?

A: Create boundaries, announce yourself as a working mother, include your family in decisions, and ask for help when you need it!

It can be easy to lose balance if you're growing a business and many opportunities are coming your way. Before you know it, your part-time job from home has turned into a 24/7 full-time job. We get it. You've grown something from nothing, and it can be difficult to say no. How you determine the amount of time to put into work is a personal decision, based on your lifestyle and perhaps your financial circumstances. It's different for everyone. Here are some signs from Audrey and Colleen to keep in mind:

FIVE SIGNS YOU'RE SPENDING TOO MUCH TIME ONLINE

1. Your four-year-old daughter asks you to please tweet the photo you just took.

2. She quickly follows that up by asking if you could also Facebook it.

3. She immediately wants to know what people commented on her photo after you post it to Facebook.

4. You can't remember the last time you got together with real-life friends.

5. You use email or Twitter as a primary form of communication with your husband.

A WEEK IN THE LIFE OF A REAL DIGITAL MOM

According to Audrey

One of the main questions I get since becoming a Digital Mom is,"What's your average week like?"

It's funny, since I've become more dedicated and devoted to my profession as a Digital Mom, my average week has become even busier. My job has changed and evolved in the last four years, but I love that I have control over my schedule. It's busy, but I need to keep it an organized busy for me and my family.

My week usually involves one trip to New York City. I'm either consulting with a company, shooting video content for someone or something, planning or working on a Getting Gorgeous event, or meeting/networking with various professionals in the social media space.

I also shoot an online TV show in Canton, Massachusetts, near Boston. So every Wednesday afternoon, I drive 45 minutes to shoot my hour-long show, then drive home.

Now an average day for me when I'm not traveling for work usually looks something like this: I wake up at 5 a.m., before anyone is up, and head downstairs to my office to write my daily blog posts (I usually write four or five a day), check my Twitter feed and Facebook accounts (both personal and work), and plan out what video I need to shoot that day for my blog. I work as the spokesperson for zulily.com (a flash sales site for parents) and write about three or four posts for them a week. Additionally, each week I have a blog and video post due for Lifetime Moms. I also contribute to a few other parenting sites, so I make sure I'm up-to-date with the content every morning. I just take this time to make sure everything is current and scheduled correctly. Once the boys are up, it's difficult to get work done with my head down because I'm constantly interrupted throughout the day, but I'm used to this now. I just make my to-do list and bang through it until it's done, even if that means being up past midnight. I also spend a good amount of time interacting and connecting on Twitter and Facebook—I fit these activities in every day because they are essential to growing my brand.

There's really never a day off in social media (although my weekends are a lot less busy because I make it a point to carve out family time). But even with my weekday schedule the way it is, working online for 12 to 14 hours a day, I love it. And with all that going on, I can still:

- drop off and pick up the boys at school any day I want.

- keep Monday and Thursday afternoons open because those are the kids' swim periods.

- attend all school and teacher meetings.

- plan my work schedule around school vacations and family gatherings.

Essentially, even with my busy schedule, I can decide when and where I'm on the job, and that's an amazing luxury to have as a working mother.

We've both been at the point where we have felt an imbalance between our family responsibilities and an unexpectedly blossoming career from home. Kelly Whalen, from The Centsible Life, offers excellent advice on the social media balancing act. She says, "The concept of balance often conjures images of a juggler for me, but in reality the middle ground is more like walking a tightrope. At times this life can seem unbalanced, but the truth is we can focus with intensity on work or children, and then make a shift based on what is happening in both worlds. Being a Digital Mom means your kids come first, and the wonderful thing about my work is it allows me to do that completely."

Now let's dive into some of our own tricks.

STRATEGIES TO KEEP WORK/LIFE BALANCE

We've already confessed to you that we've lost our balance in the past. We've also righted ourselves, so we consider ourselves experts in the field of regaining work/life balance. Here are a few key strategies we and our peers rely on and recommend you try:

Carve Out a Work Space

When you're working at the kitchen table or in the family room, it can be hard for you to concentrate if kids rule the roost (think baby gear and your teenager's dirty laundry strewn across the house). It can also be very easy for work to slowly and insidiously take over your life if the computer is constantly on and easy to access. After all, it's so easy to check incoming email messages, toggle between Facebook or Twitter, Skype a friend, or decide to just quickly post "one more thing" to your blog. To all of this, we have one word for you: danger!

Rather than trying to do all of your work at the heart of your bustling household, we recommend carving out an area in your home that is used exclusively for work. This gives you and your kids some boundaries. You go to this place to work and only to work. It's amazing what you can get done in sixty minutes with the door closed, while the kids are napping or watching a movie, compared with four hours in the middle of the living room with three kids and a smartphone.

Create a Work Schedule

The danger of this business is that you can never completely concentrate on just the kids or just the work. It's your job to define the line between the two. Make family time just that—family time—and work time, work time. You don't want to be the spouse who's always "bringing home work" (we've complained enough about that with our husbands, right?). Your kids don't need to see you always looking down at your smartphone, either. They'll start to wonder: who's more important, the text on the phone, or them? Our strategy: have at least one period in the day that is solely for the kids, preferably out of the house, where temptations to plug in are fewer, such as a playdate, the park, or swimming lessons.

Find a Way to Include Your Family in Your Work

Make work a family enterprise and involve the kids whenever you can. Maybe they can open all work-related packages or be the first to inspect the swag. Whether or not you agree with their assessments, let them weigh in on your work. Consider including them in your text, audio, or video posts. Our kids have made cameo appearances in almost all our vlogs. It makes them feel very important and validates their involvement. They love to watch the vlogs after we film them, and they enjoy seeing pictures of themselves. When we attend events or vacations that have been "sponsored" by our endeavors, we let them know that our own work has made it possible for us to enjoy these adventures. This helps the kids appreciate our work and realize that the time we spend away from the family on a business trip is a necessary part of the job.

Once you've carved out a work-only space in your house, your next challenge is to make sure that work isn't interrupted every thirty seconds by a needy toddler. We're not talking about neglect. We're talking about finding creative solutions that allow you to work while your children are happily occupied. Here are some good options to consider:

- Babysitting swaps (you work while another mom babysits; then you switch places so she can work while you watch the kids)

- Working playdates (both moms work while the kids play)

- Work date at the YMCA or your local gym, where babysitters are typically on call for a nominal fee

But no matter how much you plan ahead, sometimes it's just you at home with some very bouncy, needy kids. In these instances, you will need to incorporate your kids into the work you're doing. If that sounds impossible, trust us—it's not.

Audrey and Colleen's "Bring Your Kids to Work" Tips

1. When producing a video, include your kids interacting with the product or commenting on the story.

2. When you can, bring them to family-friendly digital events with you.

3.   Choose family-friendly content that allows them to become involved (e.g., cooking, arts and crafts, toys, sports).

4.   Have them start their own blogs, then link to their blogs from yours.

5.   Office cleanup day! Let them help you organize all your papers, supplies, and products.

6.   Field trips for your blog. Let them choose some destinations for you to blog about, then go and "report" on the experience with them.

7.   Let your kids press the keys on your computer; they'll feel that they're helping even if what they're typing is gibberish.

8.   Make a big deal out of "work lunch breaks." Just as you would go to lunch with office colleagues, do the same with your kids.

9.   Do a video chat with one of your blogging friends who has kids, and encourage the kids at both ends to chat with one another.

10.   Give the kids learning activity workbooks at the kitchen table while you answer emails (brands we like are School Zone and Kumon, or just any old activity book from the dollar store), and educational learning devices that let the kids practice their counting, reading, spatial, or comprehension skills (we love both the Leapster Explorer by Leapfrog and Vtech's MobiGo device; iPhone and its kids' apps, including the Itsy Bitsy Spider, Wheels on the Bus, the Cupcake app; and iPhone-friendly YouTube videos like *Harold and the Purple Crayon* and *Goodnight Moon*).

11.   Do arts and crafts: watercolor paint books, magazines, or glue-and-scissor art projects.

12.   Give your child a toy laptop that's "just like Mom's."

Trash Your Preconceived Notions of What It Means to Have a Professional Work Conversation

You're now a multitasking entrepreneur and mom. Life isn't perfect, and most likely many of your conference calls or working calls won't be, either. If you are a work-at-home mom with kids in the background most of the time, prepare for their voices to be heard—by everyone. Yes, kids in the background are not conducive to a good phone call. It's best to schedule the call when kids are sleeping, at preschool, or with a babysitter.

However, on some days the stars don't align and you find yourself speaking to someone rather important during that cranky 4:30 to 6 p.m. window when the kids are ravenous, loud, and out of control. Colleen once accepted a call from a PR rep during one of her two-year-old's temper tantrums. The rep offered to call back, but Colleen said, "I honestly don't see my kid's behavior exponentially improving anytime soon, so let's keep going." Colleen did her best to tame the kids, and she got through the call. Yes, she hung up exhausted and a little embarrassed, but she knew it was the best she could do. The PR rep didn't hold it against her, either. In fact, Colleen has only done more and more business for the rep in the years since.

Moms Know Best: How the Members of Our Tribe Find Balance

If you're just starting your digital life, it's probably hard to imagine that the slope is as slippery as we've described it. Trust us, it is! Every week, it seems, the *New York Times* runs another article on how the web can become an obsession, and we feel as if they're writing about us! To show you how ubiquitous and important the effort to maintain the middle ground is, we've collected a few more personal stories from our peers.

Beth Feldman, founder of RoleMommy.com and *Project You Magazine*

I have finally discovered that when your kids ask you to close down your laptop or put the BlackBerry away, it's time to listen. You will never get that time back with them, and now that mine are eight and eleven, I want them to remember me as their biggest cheerleader, tour guide, social director, chauffeur, and best friend. As for work, pursue the things you love, and learn to say no. I'm still trying to teach myself the second half of that lesson every single day!

Jo Lynne Shane, author of Musings of a Housewife.com

I cherish the fact that I can work with my four-year-old cuddled up on my lap. I try to step away from the computer when the older kids get home from school and be available to chat and make snacks. I have an office, and a desktop computer for my main computer use, so I don't always have a laptop attached to my lap, which is a good thing for me, as I tend to have a hard time unplugging.

Kristen Chase, founder of Cool Mom Picks and author of the blog Motherhood Uncensored and the book *The Mominatrix*

I have a babysitter who comes to the house two or three times a week in the mornings. I wake up early to check email and set things up for the day on my social networks, and then check in on my phone or laptop while the kids are playing or I'm out and about. I work during naptime and then generally shut things down until after bedtime, where I'll work another three or four hours. I'm fortunate that much of my work can be done without the need of full-time child care, and one reason why I did this was so I could be home with my kids. Additionally, my husband's work schedule is such that he is often gone for long stretches but then is home for long stretches, so it didn't make financial sense to hire a full-time nanny or place my kids in full-time child care. This has meant prioritizing and being vigilant about shutting things off and becoming unavailable online at certain times of the day. Given today's technology, that's quite challenging. If I find that I'm not spending enough face time with my kids, then I make sure to reevaluate and look at where I'm spending my time. If it's actual work, then great. If it's just flipping back and forth between Twitter, Facebook, and Gmail, then I force myself to stop and save that for the late evenings.

Wendy Piersall, founder of WooJr.com and author of *Mom Blogging for Dummies*

I have an advantage in that all of my children are older and in school, which means I get uninterrupted work time five days a week to do what I do. But that hasn't always been the case. When my children were younger, I either worked until 3:00 a.m. or paid for child care. It is easy to think that successful bloggers "do it all." But the most successful of us do not do it all—we have help. It may be supportive husbands or family members, or it may be hiring help with our businesses. One of the absolute hardest things I ever learned to do as an entrepreneur was ask for help. But getting help made the difference between desperate struggling and true success—both emotionally and financially.

Jyl Johnson Pattee, founder of Mom It Forward and EVO Conference

I really struggle with this, so I want to be candid that I am not the be-all, end-all on this topic. If I didn't have such a supportive

husband who's right there beside me, I don't know that it would work. I would have to choose. But since he is, and shares so much in taking care of the children, it does work. That said, one thing I'm trying to do is set aside time each day and, on a weekly basis, spend one-on-one time with each of my boys. We switch off weekly going on dates. One week I take one boy and my husband takes the other. The next week we switch. The date is all about the boys. They plan it, we do what they want (within reason), and we talk on their level. I turn the phone off, we ask each other questions, and we connect. This can be as simple as a jaunt over to a nearby park or an outing with friends and their kids at a local activity center or museum.

ARE YOU DIGITALLY ADDICTED?

There's working hard and getting the job done, and then there's digital addiction—a very specific and pernicious problem that we see strike many Digital Moms. From the pressure to succeed and the desire to be constantly in the know, to the need to tweet a status update to the tribe, check Facebook, or read multiple news sources for anything pertinent to your blog, your new online life can easily take over your real life if don't implement the strategies above.

Everyone is entitled to decide how much is too much. But unless you live on a planet where sleep isn't necessary, where kids don't need to be fed, and where messes aren't made, you probably can't be online more than eight hours a day without seriously ignoring your real life.

We feel strongly that real-life interactions need to come first, not just to prevent you from working all the time but to ensure that you stay connected each day to the vibrant world outside your computer.

Moms Know Best: Addiction Snuck In

After eleven years as an Army officer, Jenn Fowler and her husband decided it was time to make a life change. They returned to upstate New York, and Jenn stayed at home to raise the two children. She laughs that although she loved them, "Preschoolers don't have the best conversational skills." So in 2006, she turned to blogging at FrugalUpstate. com as a way to connect with other like-minded folks from the comfort of home. Blogging quickly took over her life.

Q: **What made you realize you were spending too much time online at the price of your family, hobbies, and interests?**

A: I have never felt that I spent time online at the price of my husband or kids. They do (and always will) come first. Since there is only so much time in the day, and only one of me, other things that I didn't feel were as important—such as laundry, housecleaning, and personal hobbies—did fall behind. Also, this spring a large project I had been working on fell apart. I had been mentally justifying a lot of my work and travel time as being the initial foundation work for this project. At the same time (due to other factors) my blog traffic took a huge dip, and my ad revenue slowed to a trickle. I was upset and frustrated. I felt as if I had put huge amounts of time into things that were showing me very little return. I started to feel apathetic about blogging and my online presence, yet at the same time I was scared that if I didn't keep things up I'd lose the online audience that I had spent four years building up. I felt out of balance and wasn't sure where I really wanted to go with my online life.

Q: **What actions did you take?**

A: I decided that I really needed to spend some time away—to make a complete break for a bit and give myself time to think.

I decided to take a two-week full-stop social media break. No blogging, tweeting, or Facebook posting.

Q: How did you feel when you started spending less time online?

A: It was very odd. I found myself thinking frequently at first, "Oh, this would make a funny tweet" or "That would be a good topic for a post." Since I was planting the garden, I pulled out my garden journal and spent a little extra time writing my thoughts and plans for the garden there; it was sort of a surrogate blogging experience. I also made a conscious effort to do some crafting activities that I hadn't had time to enjoy in a while.

Q: Now that you are back online, have you changed your behavior?

A: I'm online a lot less. I want to limit my online time to the activities that provide me the most bang for my buck. I decided to post infrequently this summer and then, when school starts back up, to schedule myself a set time each day for writing.

Q: How do you balance the kids when you're working from home?

A: You can't give all your attention to both your kids and a job. I think that each of us has to really sit down and prioritize their online life and presence, and then learn how to use one simple word: no.

KNOW WHEN TO SAY NO!

Busy people often lose their work/life balance because they commit themselves to more projects than they can realistically accomplish in the available time. It's particularly easy to overcommit in the sphere of social media because you could post limitless content or information if you worked 24/7. As a product review blogger, Colleen could constantly post on the latest items available for sale, just as Audrey could continually share new fashion trends or clothing styles introduced by an infinite number of designers. If you love to share details about your life and provide links to popular articles via your Facebook or Twitter accounts, you too could easily get caught up in this merry-go-round.

There's more. The busier you become, the more likely people are to ask you for just one more favor. You are already doing so much, they figure; what is one more task?

We've said this in previous chapters, but we'll say it again: you must learn to say no. No to the marketers who want you to post (for free) about their newest line of mayonnaise flavors, no to the invitation to travel to the Toyota plant with a dozen other mommy bloggers, no to the conference that wants you to speak (for free) about your expertise. Every no is a calculation; we understand that. If you say no too often, you may not get invited again. But every time you say no to a business opportunity, you are saying yes to your family, and that's a calculation we don't have to weigh or look at from a million angles. It's always going to be a right choice.

HOW TO SAY NO WITH FINESSE

We feel that the best way to decline an invitation is to be honest with the brand or company. If it's due to a family conflict, tell them. Rather than just saying "No, but thank you," it looks much better if you briefly explain the reason. For example, "Thank you so much for the invitation to your event! Unfortunately, that's the same weekend as my child's preschool play, and I just can't miss it. Please keep me in mind for any further opportunities." Short, sweet, and honest. Or—always a great option—recommend another blogger as you write back to decline.

Anytime Colleen struggles with saying no to unpaid opportunities or press events, her husband gives her a reality check. He says, "If that PR person doesn't understand why you won't work for free or don't want to fly across the country for no pay, suggest that they come fly into town and stay with our family for three days. We can give them a real feel for the experience. They can help out changing diapers, playing with the kids, grocery shopping, blogging, and more. They'll be saying no! in no time."

Last June, both of us even turned down fantastic paid opportunities because our schedules were crazy as we were writing this book while handling our family responsibilities. Audrey turned down the chance to cover an iCarly concert as a Mom Blogger correspondent, and Colleen turned down the chance to cover an event with Intel on women and technology. In both cases, it was a tough decision. The iCarly concert was in Texas—quite a hike for Audrey from Rhode Island—and she had a previous commitment. And the Intel event was in Portland, Oregon, several time zones away from Colleen's family in Philadelphia. The two-day trip would have required almost four days of babysitters, given the time it takes to fly across the country.

Sometimes what's right for one of us isn't right for the other. This year we were both invited to an exclusive private event with Pampers to discuss new products. The invitation even included a visit to the president's house for dinner. However, it was an unpaid trip. Colleen would have needed a babysitter for three days away from home, so she walked away from the opportunity. But for Audrey, it was a fit. She could arrange child care and already had an existing paid relationship with Pampers (she's a writer for the Pampers Parenting Network), and she knew this would be beneficial for her and this business arrangement.

Of course, the events that are easiest to say yes to are the ones that include our families. Give us more of those, please!

TO LOVE THE LIFE YOU LIVE, YOU NEED TO LIVE THE LIFE YOU LOVE

As we've emphasized throughout this chapter, no two moms will have the same experience trying to juggle their roles as social media maven and mom. In the end, you need to know yourself and your family. Ask yourself: How much are you willing to work? How much can your family afford for you to be away? Think from both a financial and an emotional perspective.

Our lives aren't 100 percent perfect, but we think we've found a better version of motherhood for us—one that doesn't force us to choose between staying at home and spending all of our time at the office. Digital motherhood enables us, most of the time, to do preschool pickup, play on the swing set with the kids, and create a buffet lunch of Play-Doh food with our toddlers, all while following our business passions.

By living according to our own personal values, our lives as Digital Moms reflect our own versions of what we like to think of as happily ever after. In **Step 7: Live Happily Ever After by Living Your Values,** we'll share some stories, tips, and words of wisdom from a wide range of moms who have achieved their own versions of success. If you aren't already inspired by now, these stories should give you that final little nudge you need to take your first baby steps toward your own satisfying life online.

STEP 7

Live Happily Ever After by Living Your Values

We all love a good happily-ever-after story.

When we watch movies and TV shows, we ultimately end up rooting for the characters whom we feel an emotional connection to. It's just the way we're wired. We want the couple to get together at the end. We want the good guys to prevail. We want the hard work to pay off. Is your brain doing a romantic happily-ever-after movie montage yet? We immediately think of Tom Hanks and Meg Ryan falling in love over the radio in *Sleepless in Seattle* and then all over again via email in *You've Got Mail*. We also can't help but think of Amy Adams and Meryl Streep in *Julie and Julia*. A blogger turned national sensation simply with her blog's content? Now that's happily ever after! Could something like that really happen, though? Could something that big really come from being a Digital Mom? Well . . . if you dare to dream, you never know.

Fellow blogger Katja Presnal at Skimbaco.com sums it up well: "Only a crazy person would dream that she could work from home sitting on the couch most days, and then when she gets out of the house, work with celebrities, attend events, meet with Fortune 500 CEOs in boardrooms, and fly around the country to write about travel destinations or meet with corporate clients."

Of course, as we've said all along, there will be different ideal endings for everyone.

Colleen realized she was living happily ever after this summer. She was seated beside her four-year-old daughter, who suddenly shouted out, "Today is the best day ever!" Were they at Disney World? No. They were at the local mall, filled to the brim with Chick-fil-A and milkshakes, enjoying a play date at an art studio. Colleen's daughter held in her hand what may have been the world's ugliest bird house—a beautified coffee can. But Colleen agreed with her. It was the best day. The week before, Colleen had been walking a tightrope, trying to fit in three TV segments and a trip to San Diego. Exhausted, she came back determined to right the scales for her family and herself. And she did. Hearing "Today is the best day ever" from her daughter is what it's all about—her version of a happily ever after.

For Audrey, happily ever after began with an email. She read it a hundred times before she believed it. "Me? On a fashion panel for the People's Choice Awards? Speaking on camera with Tim Gunn? Are you absolutely, positively sure?" She'd finally expanded her platform enough to get herself to be recognized as *the* mom fashion expert, but was this really where that had led? One month later, there she was, chatting with Tim Gunn in Los Angeles at the Kodak Theatre. "Donna Karan this," she said; "Project Runway that," he said—a regular conversation—when, midsentence, he said, "Wait—are you Audrey, Audrey the mommy blogger that is joining us on the fashion panel?" Audrey laughed. "But you're a fresh breath of air! Welcome!" Gunn exclaimed. Who knows what he was expecting from a mom blogger. But she loved how it made her feel. He knew that she knew what she was talking about. She belonged there.

That's the best part about being a Digital Mompreneur—you get to personally shape the happily ever after you desire. Whether it's working from home, spending more time with your children, financially contributing to the household, paying for a babysitter, committing to a cause, being the sole provider in the household, finally feeling a true passion for your work, not commuting a gazillion hours to and from work, or, in the case of Laurie Turk at tipjunkie.com, devising a digital business that pays off an astronomical medical bill. What motivates you? Perhaps it's a combination of a few things.

This book has attempted to walk you down the path toward happily ever after. You may get there as soon as you receive your first comment. You may get there when you have 10,000 daily visitors to your site. You may get there when Rachael Ray emails you about one of your authentic French recipes. But to get there you must begin!

To review, here are the steps:

Step 1: Find your passion

Step 2: Hang a digital "shingle" and start typing

Step 3: Find your tribe

Step 4: Make opportunity knock and learn how to answer that door

Step 5: Manage the Benjamins

Step 6: Don't forget the children! (Define your version of success and make sure you're truly on middle ground)

Step 7: Live happily ever after by living your values

In each of those steps, we shared "Moms Know Best" stories from our digital friends that were meant to advise and inspire you. But we think we've saved the best stories for last. In the remainder of this chapter we take you into the homes, offices, conference calls, inboxes, and Twitter accounts of Digital Moms who've made it in one way or another. In other words, we take you up close. From here on out, think of yourself as flies on the wall of happily ever after. Is any inspiration better than that? We don't think so.

Alicia Voorhies

A Digital Mom at www.thesoftlanding.com (store) and www.thesoftlandingbaby.com (blog)

Wired since: 2007

Proudest accomplishment as a Digital Mom: I'm so pleased to have been a part of the grassroots movement that insisted manufacturers remove BPA (Bisphenol A) from baby bottles and feeding gear—even when our federal regulators didn't see the need.

Moment you knew you were on the right track: I knew I'd stepped into the perfect career when my first blog reader called to thank me for making her burden as a parent so much lighter by researching toxic plastic in everyday products so she didn't have to.

Most flattering comment: My all-time favorite compliment came from Ken Cook, president of Environmental Working Group (EWG) and my favorite toxic chemical reform activist, who said he always checks my product research before purchasing anything for his son!

Happiest moment recently: I was relaxing with my laptop on the beach during our family vacation, watching my husband and kids play in the ocean, when it hit me: I get to work alongside my amazing family, my job is built around a lifelong passion for alternative health, and I'm able to work from anywhere in the world, which allows me to homeschool my children. Could it get any better?

Websites you couldn't live without: ewg.org, healthychild. org, saferchemicals.org, chej.org, mercola.com, natural-news.com, blog.beliefnet.com/moviemom, smartbrief.com, chrisbrogan.com

Perfect day: Waking up to watch the sunrise on a family camping trip, followed by swimming, fishing, and walks around the lake. I'd steal an hour or two to get a blog post written and end the day with my favorite people around a blazing campfire.

Sarah Welch

A Digital Mom at GetButtonedUp.com

Wired since: 2004

Proudest accomplishment as a Digital Mom: My proudest accomplishment as a Digital Mom is having played a part in creating something meaningful from scratch.

Moment you knew you were on the right track: At the very beginning, when the four of us were just talking about this idea, we learned that Buttoned Up could be trademarked—we all got goose bumps.

Most flattering comment: "Thank you for the awakening. Peace to you." It was a comment posted on a story I wrote about organizing yourself to live a meaningful life. It's always nice to know that the things you are writing and creating actually reach and mean something to people.

Happiest moment recently: There have been so many great moments, it's hard to pick. I suppose it really comes down to something that I get to experience almost every day, and that is hearing my four-year-old son's footsteps racing toward my home office door at about 3 p.m. and being able to greet him with a big hug and have a nice chat. I also love that I am "still at work" and yet can start prepping dinner around 4:30 p.m. My favorite moment with him happened a month or so ago. I was on the phone with a buyer from the world's largest retailer, and my son was "taking notes" on his Superman notepad next to me. When the call was over, we celebrated with a little happy dance.

Websites you couldn't live without: Blogs.BabyCenter. com, Facebook.com, Twitter.com, TheScramble.com, blog.mrslilien.com.

Perfect day: Wake up at 5:45 and get in a good workout before the boys wake up, preferably by going for a run outside. Eat breakfast as a family, play Hotwheels for a bit afterward, then get everybody dressed and ready for the day. Check email and do work after boys head to school. Shower around 9:30 a.m. Work until lunch. Grab noon train into the city for a meeting, and sneak in a visit with a friend in the late afternoon. Express train home at 4 p.m. In the door by 5:15. Make dinner with computer "cookbook." Eat dinner as a family. Walk down to the beach after dinner and play in the sand with the guys—and maybe meet up with a few good friends there. Walk home. Put boys to bed at 7:30 or 8:00. Catch up with Gar. Watch the latest *Grey's Anatomy* (or *Entourage* or *Real Housewives)*. Read for fifteen to twenty minutes. Lights out at 10:30.

Tamara Walker

A Digital Mom at MomRN.com and Ask MomRN Show (www.MomRN.com and www.blogtalkradio.com/MomRN)

Wired since: 2001 and 2008, respectively

Proudest accomplishment as a Digital Mom: Helping others through my own expertise as a mom, nurse, and child safety expert and bringing the expertise of others to my audience.

Moment you knew you were on the right track: I knew I was on the right track when one of my website visitors emailed me to tell me how much my advice had helped her and her family overcome a very difficult parenting challenge.

Most flattering comment: I was interviewing Kathy Ireland, and she interrupted me to praise my work and thank me for the important service I provide. I was blown away, because she is someone I admire very much for her own work in helping others!

Happiest moment recently: A few months ago, my husband and I had a heart-to-heart talk. Our daughter had just graduated from high school, and since we'd home-schooled her, I had not been working outside the home. I wanted to help our finances by getting a job, but my husband told me he was so proud of what I do as "Mom-RN" and wanted me to continue to work toward making that my full-time job. He was afraid it would suffer if I worked outside the home. I cried happy tears because I love what I get to do and how I get to serve others as "MomRN" and would love to build it into a full-time career! My husband has always been my number-one supporter and fan, and I could never do any of this without him!

Websites you couldn't live without: FlyLady.net, Mom-Spark.net

Perfect day: Spending a day with my family and friends just talking and having fun!

Ellen Seidman

A Digital Mom at Love That Max (http://lovethatmax.com)

Wired since: 2009

Proudest accomplishment as a Digital Mom: Creating an inspirational, informational, occasionally irreverent community for moms of kids with special needs . . . and being named a Top 50 Mom Blog by Babble in 2010.

Moment you knew you were on the right track: When I started getting emails from moms telling me how much my blog helped them through their darkest hours—and made them laugh.

Most flattering comment: "You are my Internet Energizer Bunny inspiration."

Happiest moment recently: My son, who has cerebral palsy and has a lot of trouble speaking, was jealous that his little sister had gotten a new bed and said the words "Big boy bed" to me. *Anytime* my son talks, it's bliss-inducing.

Websites you couldn't live without: The Bloggess (www.thebloggess.com), because she makes me laugh every single time; People.com, because I need to be fed daily celeb fluff; the "Blog" of "Unnecessary" Quotation Marks (www.unnecessaryquotes.com), because I too am a grammar geek.

Perfect day: Sleep late, play with kids (who don't fight), sushi with husband (must include spicy tuna roll), shopping trip in which all clothes I try on fit, nap in afternoon (see a pattern here?), dinner party with friends, fire in fireplace, watch Letterman in bed with husband, kids do not sneak into bed in middle of night. The end.

Jamie Reeves

A Digital Mom at www.blondemomblog.com

Pontificating about poop and pinot noir since 2005

Proudest accomplishment as a Digital Mom: As a mother to two young daughters, being chosen to work on social media campaigns that send powerful messages to young girls, such as the American Girl parent partners, Shine On Now program, and Dove's Self-Esteem movement.

Moment you knew you were on the right track: When I realized that blogging was more than a hobby for me. Now I understand that it's both an important creative outlet and an incredible networking tool that has introduced me to fascinating people and places!

Most flattering comment: One of my readers recently admitted to me that she didn't know what she'd do without me and her hairdresser! *The Tennessean*, the newspaper of my hometown city of Nashville, also featured me on their blog in March 2010, saying, "Blonde mom writes so charmingly about her family life, which also includes her high-school sweetheart husband, two dogs, one fish, and 'too much laundry,' that you might find yourself falling a little in love with her, in between those laugh-out-loud posts."

Happiest moment recently: Last summer my entire family was invited to St. Augustine and Ponte Vedra Beach, Florida, to review a local hotel and family tourism attractions. My husband lived in that area for three years before we got engaged. He absolutely fell in love with it and still misses it to this day. It was so incredible to be able to travel back to the area he loves so much with our daughters and share the beach and beautiful area with them— all thanks to my blog. We strolled down A1A, wandered the cobblestone streets of historic St. Augustine, and saw where my husband worked and lived before moving back to Nashville. It was an awesome homecoming for him, and he got to share it with us!

Websites you couldn't live without: www.weather.com (I am a huge weather nerd), www.etsy.com (I'm an Etsy-holic), and www.cnn.com (I monitor the news for my day job).

Perfect day: A big Southern-style breakfast with my family and then spending time totally getting away from it all with the three most important people in my life, which includes staying unplugged from Twitter and all those shiny pretty apps on my iPhone. There's no app for the perfect day!

Corine Ingrassia

A Digital Mom at ComplicatedMama.com and TheBigToy-Book.com

Wired since: 2008 and 2010, respectively

Proudest accomplishment as a Digital Mom: Receiving my LLC for my freelancing business.

Moment you knew you were on the right track: When I was receiving a paycheck for doing something that was flexible for my family and allowed me to connect with other Moms who have gone on to be some of my closest friends. Anytime you love what you do, you are on the right track.

Most flattering comment: When I am asked by other moms how I do what I do, and how they can do it too. There is no feeling like feeling that I've inspired someone else.

Happiest moment recently: As moms we are always seeking that perfect balance; being a Digital Mom is no different. As flexible as my schedule is, I still have to put in some late nights to make deadlines or take days away to cover an event. The difference for me has been that my kids don't have to wait for "take your child to work day" to see what their mom does. They see me writing at home, and many times they are invited to attend the events I'm covering. Last year my family and I were invited to several live events, including the Radio City Christmas Spectacular, which has always been a family tradition for us. Through my involvement in social media and specifically with the Big Toy Book, my children are also often called for Toy segments and print work, and they love it because it's all toys and all fun. This past month when my son posed for the cover of the "Toy

Insider" for *Woman's Day* magazine, he was treated like a celebrity and beamed ear to ear. When the shoot was over and he got to take home a toy he had been eyeing the whole time, he looked at me and said, "Mom, that was so fun! Can I take my new toy for show and tell this week?"

Websites you couldn't live without: Daily Candy, TMZ, Mashable, Twitter, Facebook, and Google. Does Google count? Because I definitely couldn't live without it.

Perfect day: Consists of a to-do list completed during nap time, an empty laundry room, and watching a movie with the family.

Kristen Howerton

A Digital Mom at Rage Against the Minivan (www.rage againsttheminivan.com)

I am also editor of the parenting e-zine Mama Manifesto (www.mamamanifesto.com).

Wired since: 2004

Proudest accomplishment as a Digital Mom: Being chosen as a Voice of the Year Finalist the first year I attended BlogHer, and getting to talk about adoption on *The View* after a producer read my blog.

Moment you knew you were on the right track: When I was wanting to write more than I wanted to do my day job (as a psychotherapist). I had always heard the adage "do what you love," but I never imagined that I could love my job. Now that I have moved into writing full time, I get it.

Most flattering comment: Several people have told me that I've inspired them to adopt. That means the world to me.

Happiest moment recently: I recently got to spend a weekend at a retreat with thirty-five bloggers I admire. It was an amazing experience, both personally and professionally. It was a weekend full of food, wine, connecting, and late-night conversations. Magic happens when a bunch of brainy women get together, and I loved being able to absorb it all. There was side-splitting laughter, and insane vulnerability, and the comfort of being understood. Ultimately it was a group of women honestly grappling with the balance between being a fully present mom and a woman with other passions, and I walked away feeling inspired.

Websites you couldn't live without: I love ShePosts.com for covering the breadth of the mommy-blogging world in one place. I love The Onion, Dooce, and Mamapop for my daily laughs.

Perfect day: My perfect day would involve a little me time and a little family time. Probably a morning at the spa, a little time to write in a quiet space, and then an afternoon and evening with my family.

Cecily Kellogg

A Digital Mom at UppercaseWoman.com and CecilyK.com

Wired since: 2004 and 2010, respectively

Proudest accomplishment as a Digital Mom: Discovering for sure that I am a writer.

Moment you knew you were on the right track: When the words I wrote began to sing.

Most flattering comment: Okay, this is going to sound grandiose, but there have been thousands. Literally. But I did have a favorite tweet: the person said, "I believe in you and your writing, and I would buy your book" (I don't yet have a book).

Happiest moment recently: I recently spoke at a small blogging conference about "finding your voice," and it was so amazingly well received—over nine pages of tweets while I spoke, and thirty blog entries after—that I felt truly accomplished as a speaker and writer. But having my daughter grab my face to direct me to look at something she's done feels just as amazing.

Websites you couldn't live without: Google. My email is through Google, my feed reader, my analytics, my feed burner . . . but blogs? My husband's, my best friend's, Dooce (www.dooce.com), A Little Pregnant (www.alittlepregnant.com), and about 500 more.

Perfect day: Sleeping until I wake up, and having a happy and entertained kid all day. Or, sleeping until I wake up and then cooking breakfast over a campfire. Or, sleeping until I wake up and having the day just with my husband. So, basically, any day that includes sleep.

Beth Feldman

A Digital Mom at Role Mommy, *Project You Magazine*, and Lifetime Mom

Wired since: 2006, 2010, and 2009, respectively

Proudest accomplishment as a Digital Mom: Helping other Digital Moms achieve their goals as writers, authors, and entrepreneurs.

Moment you knew you were on the right track: When my dream to launch *Project You Magazine* (an ezine for parents) finally came to fruition and we garnered more than 30,000 views in two weeks. All I can say is, "Hallelujah!"

Most flattering comment: From @mominthecity Kimberly Coleman: "It's @rolemommy's birthday! #followfriday her because the world is a better place for having her in it!"

Happiest moment recently: Recently, my husband sent me a text message that read, "I am so proud of all that you have accomplished and I love you very much." It's wonderful to pursue your passion and achieve success, but for me, the biggest joy in this adventure has been that my husband and kids have been an important part of the journey.

Websites you couldn't live without: Google, Facebook, Twitter, Fresh Direct.

Perfect day: My recent birthday. Breakfast in bed prepared by my kids and husband. Lunch with incredible Digital Moms: Katja Presnal (www.skimbaco.com), Jen Singer (www.mommasaid.net), Dawn Sandomeno (www.partybluprintsblog.com), and Elizabeth Mascali (www.

partybluprintsblog.com). A doubles tennis game with neighborhood friends, a romantic dinner with my husband at one of the places we used to visit when we were dating, tons of messages on my Facebook page wishing me a happy birthday, and the chance to reconnect with old friends by phone and text message. I wish every day was my birthday—without the aging part, of course.

Jen Singer

A Digital Mom at MommaSaid.net

Wired since: 2003

Proudest accomplishment as a Digital Mom: Seeing my site turn into a three-book series.

Moment you knew you were on the right track: When I got on CBS's *The Early Show* in 2005.

Most flattering comment: Moms email me every now and then to tell me I made them laugh and feel better about themselves on a rough day (or week/month/year).

Happiest moment recently: Every single time people respond to my post-PET scan tweets, which usually go like this: "JenSinger must quote Springsteen: 'Ain't no sin to be glad you're alive.'" "No cancer . . . again. All clear!"

Websites you couldn't live without: Mom-101, Parenting. com, Facebook, Hootsuite, MommaSaid (of course).

Perfect day: Any day I get to write.

Amy Oztan

Digital Mom at SelfishMom.com, BloggingAngels.com, and NYCMetroMoms.com

Wired since: 2008, 2010, and coming soon!

Proudest accomplishment as a Digital Mom: Being able to help other moms understand that they're not the only ones with messy houses, bratty kids, piles of laundry, headaches, screaming fits, and all the rest of the crap that goes along with being an imperfect (and perfectly normal) mom.

Moment you knew you were on the right track: When commenters started saying things like "OMG, I thought I was the only one! I'm so happy I read this."

Most flattering comment: One Blogging Angels podcast listener said recently that she listens to each one twice to make sure she gets all the info. That made me feel great, because I've always hated my speaking voice, but if she's been listening twice it can't be that bad!

Happiest moment recently: I was making a video with my kids to promote a product, and the video involved my daughter painting my son with food. We all had a blast, and they were adorable. While editing it, I thought back over the past few years of blogging that had gotten me to the point where my kids were playing with food on camera and I was being paid to have fun recording it. It's still unbelievable to me that this is my job!

Websites you couldn't live without: Mom-101.com, because she's a gifted and funny writer and never goes for the cheap shot to get a point across, and Fark.com, because somewhere inside of me is a twelve-year-old boy who loves completely inappropriate jokes.

Perfect day: Sleeping in late, getting a massage, spending some time with my family, then kicking them all out so I can get some work done. I'm always so behind, and it makes me feel great to check things off my many to-do lists!

Moms Know Best: The Power of Social Media

Dawn Sandomeno, cofounder of the Partybluprints.com blog and coauthor of *Plan to Party,* published in 2010, has found great success by immersing herself in social media. We asked her how social media had made it possible for her to publish her book.

The idea for Plan to Party *truly grew into a reality from the seeds we planted in the social media space. The seeds were our blog and our genuine and active engagement and presence on Twitter and Facebook. Writing a book was always our plan, but it happened much sooner than we expected. We recognized that the book was a great way to reach an audience outside of the blog and another medium through which we could inspire people to entertain.*

The first spark for the book came via Twitter, when I connected with @PublishingGuru, Todd Rutherford. Todd is VP of Yorkshire Publishing; he is active on Twitter and values the space and its potential. We followed each other and started tweeting, and soon our relationship progressed, along with the idea of publishing a book together. Then the idea became a reality when Elizabeth took over the reins and spent months designing, developing, and turning our content into Plan to Party.

I laugh to myself when I hear pundits dismiss the power of Twitter and social media. For us it has opened so many doors that otherwise would have been not only closed but unknown to us. Social media have the unique ability to remove barriers of time, space, and perception in a way that I think is wonderful and should be respected. I have had the opportunity to tweet with Deepak Chopra about advice for my insomnia, to meet new and wonderful women I now consider good friends, and to know those in our area of expertise. Women like Jeanne Benedict, whom we met via Twitter and Facebook. Jeanne, a well-known lifestyle and party expert, TV host, and author, ended up writing the foreword for our book.

As you can see, being a Digital Mom right now is a bit like being on the frontier. Where the land ends, no one knows. And we don't see that changing anytime soon. Every year, new bloggers enter the "hall of fame," skyrocketing to the top of the charts with thousands of followers. And every year, midsize bloggers continue to double their traffic; others grow in influence as niche experts; and still others become go-to social media experts for brands and Fortune 500 companies. And every year, tiny blogs, just starting up with the quietest of peeps, have the potential to become über-blogs that enter the hall of fame in the months and years to come.

In short, we feel there will always be room for new bloggers to join in and gain popularity. Just like we all welcome new TV shows, novels, and movies each year, we are always looking to be entertained or inspired by someone with a fresh angle and voice. And bloggers are a constantly evolving source of both.

THE FUTURE

With our evolution will come changes to how we earn money and how much we earn. We think the corporate world is still figuring out how valuable we are as messengers of goodwill and good products. As spokespeople and brand ambassadors, we will *always* cost less than celebrities, and every day there's more proof that we are more effective at dispensing news and messages than famous faces ever were. Our targeted messages hit home because we're real moms and ordinary people. To wit: what's more powerful, a Tide commercial filled with unfamiliar faces that runs on Fox during an NFL football game, or the hilarious mommy blogger you're obsessed with who happened to use Tide to get dirt out of her kid's baseball uniform?

We're even willing to bet that some rival companies may soon hold bidding wars over Digital Moms who hold great sway and influence in the blogosphere. Imagine how much influence one Digital Mom could have as a spokesperson if she had thousands upon thousands of moms hanging on her every word or tweet? How much would you pay her to talk about your product, brand, favorite show, or household appliance?

Well, she exists. And new versions of her pop up every day.

For those of us with slightly less power and sway, there is still a great upside. We have changed the employer/employee dynamic forever. Our value and our expertise are manifest not through our résumés, but through our daily action and interactions. We are not standing still, waiting for something to happen. We are making something happen each day. It gives us power: the power of our connections, the power of our words, the power of real value.

And maybe, by our examples, workplace managers will finally acknowledge the great disconnect between motherhood and career that has made life so confusing and hard for so many women over the past fifty years. There is nothing right or reasonable about a forty-hour work week outside the house for a mother of two, let alone a mother of four. We'd be thrilled if the result of all this Digital Mom success could be a reflexive change in the way offices operate, including flexible work options that allow qualified women to work any hours they want so long as the work gets done. Not that we want to lose any moms from our tribe. But we sure would love to see more happy working moms living balanced lives. And if we are a model for how that's possible, and that model leads to women going back to work because work outside the home is suddenly viable, so be it.

But to get this movement moving, you must join it. The beginning, middle, and end of your particular Digital Mom story will ultimately revolve around how much time you choose to invest and how far you want your journey to go. We've seen magic happen online. We've seen dreams come true. We've seen lives change. We're examples of how it can happen to you in this incredible digital space. So, please, go for it! After all, let's face it, at the ending of all of our stories, it would be nice to have it read: "and they all lived happily ever after."

Parting Words

As we first mentioned back in the introduction, blogging has truly changed our lives.

For Audrey, starting an online business helped her take an active role after her husband was laid off from work during the economic downturn. Like so many moms out there, she needed to step up and take over, and, through hard work, she's been able to sustain her family. In fact, the business has been so successful that Audrey's husband joined her MomGenerations.com team and now helps her run the business from home with the boys. It's become their true family business—the ultimate dream come true for her.

For Colleen, what started as a window to the outside world from her laptop during the isolating stages of new motherhood has evolved into an exciting life and career she never imagined. From meeting her all-time favorite movie star, Jennifer Garner, to sailing on the Disney Dream Cruise ship maiden voyage with her family, being a Digital Mom has allowed her to balance her life as a suburban mom with a touch of Hollywood glam and to use her MBA skills on a daily basis. And all of this is happening while being able to stay true to her goal of striking the right balance between her family and a career.

If we achieve this, so can you, and the best advice we can give is to give yourself time to enjoy your new friends online, your bustling business, and your rapidly growing children. And remember that we went through everything you're going through, too.

We hope that our book has given you the basics—and the inspiration—you need to get started, as well as some advice to make your digital journey easier. At the end of this book you'll also find the **Crash Course in Social Media** (if you haven't already read it or would like a refresher), a list of some excellent blogs by moms for you to check out, and some references that might be helpful as you take your first digital steps.

We look forward to hearing about your digital journey. If you ever have questions, comments, ideas, or want to say hi, please look us up on Twitter, Facebook, or our blogs. We welcome the conversation. We'll do our best to respond or share the comments and ideas on our blog (but like many of you, our lives are a juggling act and those little kids keep us busy!). We hope to meet you virtually or in real life soon.

Digitally Yours,

Audrey and Colleen

P.S. Here are our Twitter handles again.

You can find Audrey here: @audreymcclellan

You can find Colleen here: @classymommy

Appendix A

A CRASH COURSE IN SOCIAL MEDIA

To build an audience or grow a business in today's digital world, you need to understand and properly use social media. While many sites fall under that umbrella term, for the sake of this crash course we'll focus on the most important platforms for you to experiment with. Here they are in order of importance:

A Twitter account

A personal Facebook page

A Facebook fan page for your blog or business

A YouTube account

A LinkedIn account

In the following pages, we'll examine each of these platforms, explaining why you should use it, how you should use it, and the basics you need to get started. We'll devote extra time to Twitter and Facebook because in our experience, they offer the greatest potential for building your online profile. If used effectively, these social media giants can not only grow your business but also provide the opportunity for you to become a consultant for, or even manage, the social media efforts of larger companies that don't understand technology as well as you do.

Now we recognize that many Digital Moms have signed on to these tools already. However, we believe that they'll also benefit from this refresher because they often aren't using these social media platforms to their full potential. And if you aren't actively engaging, communicating, promoting, and making relationships, you're missing out on a fantastic opportunity to grow your tribe.

Twitter

What It Is

Twitter is a microblogging tool, which means that it is just like the blogging you already do, except that you are limited to 140 characters with each post, or tweet. It's also a bit like instant messaging, but with many more people potentially listening to what you have to say.

Why You Use It

Twitter allows you to share information and gives you real-time access to all the people with whom you've connected. For example, if you have 1,000 followers on Twitter (which is not hard to achieve) and you post that you're seeking a recipe for baked French toast, get ready—you'll have a recipe in seconds. If you want everyone to know about your recent house purchase, prepare for hundreds of "hurrays" and possibly a few "send a picture" and "is your home for sale?" messages. Twitter opens your world up to millions of moms, brands, and companies.

Tweeter-extraordinaire Amy Lupold Bair of Resourceful Mommy says it best: "In high school I was friends with the drama geeks, the jocks, the student council nerds, and the slackers, but I could never hang out with them in the same place. Twitter is that place. I can be friends with people from all parts of the world and all walks of life and talk to them all at the same time. In short, Twitter is the ultimate in helping you connect and spread any and all messages you want to get into the online space."

How to Get Started

First, head over to Twitter.com and use the instructions to create a profile. Next, review the Twitter terminology below. Start "following" some friends, celebrities, brands, companies. Then dive into our tips on how to truly get the most out of this amazing tool.

Twitter Terminology

DM (a.k.a. Direct Message) A DM is a private message of 140 characters or less sent to a fellow Twitter follower. DMs are great because they are private real-time messages. Use this option when you don't want all of your followers to see the message you send. This is an example of Audrey DM'ing Colleen. Notice that we insert a small "d" in front of the Twitter handle; this is how you "direct message" someone on Twitter.

d classymommy Do you have a contact for someone at Macy's?

d audreymcclellan Yes, just emailed you the contact I have!

Dming is a great tool because it allows for quick and fast interaction with results.

Followers Followers are any other Twitter users who might stumble across you and ask to be part of your network. They see all your tweets and can respond to them if they so choose. The number of your followers can be very important when you reach out to companies for business opportunities.

Handle A handle is the name you select for your profile on Twitter, and it becomes part of your Twitter URL (Uniform Resource Locater). In other words, you can be found at www.twitter.com/handle; in Audrey's case, at www.twitter.com/AudreyMcClellan.

Your Twitter handle can be only sixteen characters long, and when you pick it, you may need to be creative because no two people can have the same handle. Also, use "Mom" if possible and try to keep it simple enough for people to remember it easily. Colleen (@ClassyMommy), for example, uses the name of her blog to make it simple for people to find and follow her.

Hashtag So many Twitter conversations are going on at any given moment that a hashtag (#) is used to help people keep within a common conversation or topic. For example, if you're on Twitter and discussing *Project Runway* with other people watching the show, you would label all of your tweets with #projectrunway. It's a great way to easily search topics on Twitter, too. Particularly helpful searches for Digital Moms might be #breastfeeding, #homeschool, and #bloggingmoms. When you first start out, get in the habit of following hashtags because they help you follow conversations more easily and, in turn, meet other tweeters who like to tweet about the same topics as you. Feel free at any point to start your own, too!

Hootsuite Hootsuite is a social media dashboard that allows you to connect to multiple social networks from one place. A dashboard allows you to manage many accounts from one spot. It's great for connecting you to Twitter, Facebook, and LinkedIn from one place. Hootsuite helps you stay organized and save time, which allows you to plan a better social media strategy.

Listed Twitter started Lists to allow fellow tweeters to organize their followers in an easier fashion. You may create lists any way you like. You could make a list for fellow tweeters in your area. You could make a list of brands and companies you want to follow on Twitter. Or you could create a list filled with something as simple as your favorite tweeters. It's a great way to keep everything readily accessible.

Reply This is how you respond to a tweet. You always have to include the @ sign when you're replying to someone. The @ sign is the address, so to speak, of the person you're sending the message to. It's very simple.

Retweet (a.k.a. RT) A retweet is reposting a tweet you have seen on Twitter to your own followers on Twitter. It is essential that you give credit to the originator when you retweet something. An RT that would serve a Digital Mom might be something like this: "RT @AudreyMcClellan HUGE SALE on Crocs for Kids right now on Zulily!" In this case, Audrey originally shared the message with all of her followers, including Colleen. Now Colleen is sharing this message with all of her followers and giving Audrey credit for the post. By doing so, she recognizes Audrey's original contribution.

Search.Twitter.com This website is the place to search for things on Twitter. You can search by hashtag or just by keyword, as you would on Google. A perfect example of a beneficial search is #breastcancerawareness. You will see all the tweets that mention this topic and be able to find resources from there.

Trending Topics Twitter posts the most popular topics of the day. Usually they reflect the top news stories. For example, around the time of elections, the topics all trended to candidates and results. When Eva Longoria and Tony Parker broke up, there were trending topics about that. When the Super Bowl is on, there are trending topics about that as well. These topics change daily, so it's always interesting to check in and see what's trending.

Tweet A tweet is a post or status update that is 140 characters or less. If you would like to include a fellow tweeter in your message, you must include the @ symbol, followed by the person's handle. So, for example, if Audrey is tweeting Colleen, she will tweet, "Wondering what @ClassyMommy is doing today." Here's another example of a tweet exchange (Colleen tweeting Audrey): "@AudreyMcClellan what books worked for you the best when potty training the boys?" And then Audrey would tweet back, "Oh, @ClassyMommy, I loved the boys' version of "'Once Upon a Potty!'"

TweetDeck TweetDeck is a free application for Twitter that allows you to easily organize and update your followers, your replies, your direct messages, and your lists. We both love using TweetDeck on our iPhones and our laptops at home. It lays out Twitter in a very organized way, which allows you to keep track of tweets and DMs at the same time.

Tweet Grid Tweet Grid is a popular and user-friendly application to use for Twitter Parties because you can easily do Twitter searches that update in real time. It's a great way to do business with Twitter because you can follow many people at once.

Twitter Party (a.k.a Tweet-Up) This is a real-time virtual party that takes place online. The tweeters attending the Twitter Party are all asked to use the same hashtag (defined by the Twitter Party host), so tweeters can determine who is involved in the party and who is not. Participating in a Twitter Party is easier if you use a platform like TweetChat.com or TweetGrid.com that lets you see all the tweets relating to the party. For example, a party about Kodak's new camera might use the hashtag #NewKodak. Twitter parties are fabulous! You have the opportunity to meet tons of new people at once. Every time we participate or host a Twitter Party our number of followers increases. We suggest attending these parties once a month because they help you get out there and become more immersed in the world of Twitter.

Tinyurl.com or Bit.ly Both of these websites let you shorten any website address. Just type in the URL, and a supershort one will pop up that redirects you to the desired site. Without either of these services, getting those links into your 140-character Twitter posts would be nearly impossible! We suggest you tweet all of your blog posts, and the only way you can do that is to make the URL tiny. We tweet our daily blog posts all the time, and we do the same for our blogging friends. It's a great way to grab some traffic for your blog from Twitter.

Getting the Most Out of Twitter

Your main goal with Twitter is to gain followers. To do that, you must first follow others. To seek out someone specific, use the Twitter search tool. This function can make your Twitter experience exponentially more successful. For example, if you are watching TV alone during a hit show and search "Glee" or #Glee, you'll find what everyone is saying about it. If you want to see who is talking about the oil spill in the Gulf and type in "oil spill," you'll get a real-time feed of any tweets using those words, whether or not you follow those people. This allows you to connect with those who share your interests and enables you to engage with them.

Beyond searching for events to follow, you might try looking up and following brands or companies you love, other bloggers whose websites you like to read (usually bloggers have their Twitter handles on their websites), news sites, and even celebrities (this won't necessarily help your business, but it will give you an excuse to check your Twitter feed when you're feeling lazy—and that check may lead to a connection with someone who can help your digital business grow).

Once you're following some people, start conversations. Give an @reply when a topic interests you. You don't have to be a poet. In 140 characters nobody expects articulate conversations. However, don't just tell everyone you made your kids peanut butter and jelly for lunch. When you're planning to tweet original posts, keep in mind that your content needs to be interesting to *other* Twitter users. Link to an article that you find interesting in the *Wall Street Journal or Parenting.* Point your followers to a blog post that made you laugh out loud. Give them the inside scoop on coupon deals. Make them feel that you get interesting information in front of their eyes before anyone else. They'll love you for it. More than anything, though, be meaningful with your tweets, and think about providing as much as you are consuming.

On the other hand, if you read someone else's great tweet and believe that forwarding it will serve your followers' interests (and your own), retweet it. Who doesn't like a compliment? News stories, someone's success story, a request for help, a product review—these are all retweetable. Chances are if you liked reading that article or hearing that news, someone else will too.

If other people reply to or retweet your posts, keep the conversations going. Before you know it, you'll have even more followers, and it's very likely those followers will follow you back to your blog or wherever else your digital business resides.

When you're feeling particularly Twitter savvy, try doing the following to enhance your Twitter experience:

- **Participate in Twitter events.** Some good ones include Girls Night Out #GNO on Tuesday evenings, Twitter Parties with brands and companies, and those held by Resourceful Mommy (http://resource-fulmommy.com/) or Social Moms (socialmoms.com). These parties help narrow the Twitter universe to just moms or just women, so that if you start a conversation you'll know it's within a pool of somewhat familiar characters, all of whom may be interested in your digital business. If you feel a little intimidated coming to the party "alone," feel free to check out www.digitalmomhandbook.com or our Twitter and Facebook feeds, where we'll help you keep track of some good events to join.

- **Think geography.** We believe that real-life interactions take your life and your business to new levels. Find tweeters in your area by using the Twellow Pages (www.twellow.com).

- **Use Twitter to build your Rolodex.** Use Twitter to find PR contacts or companies you might need to reach. When Audrey was looking for an L.L. Bean contact, she just contacted the company on Twitter, and they immediately put her in touch with the go-to source she needed. Twitter can also put you in touch with customer service reps when you are desperate. Such connections can help launch your Digital Mom business.

- **Develop relationships with companies you like:** Compliment companies directly when you have a great customer service experience with them, and complain when you don't (sometimes you'll get a discount on future products). Either way, smart companies are realizing that they need to interact directly with consumers about their experience. Use that new understanding to gain advantage as a consumer and also to get your blogs and comments in front of companies that might be interested in you.

Facebook

What It Is

It's hard to imagine anyone asking "What is Facebook?" anymore, but for all the millions who are signed up (about 500 million right now), there are millions who are not—and that could be you. Facebook is essentially an up-to-the-minute yearbook page that's all about you. ("The name of the service stems from the colloquial name of books given to students at the start of the academic year by university administrations in the United States with the intention of helping students to get to know each other better," according to Wikipedia).

Why You Use It

Facebook is a remarkable tool that you can use to connect to friends, family, acquaintances, and professional contacts, both for business and for personal reasons.

Let's start with the personal side of Facebook—your personal page. At the most basic level, you use it to connect with friends and family. When you update it, you allow your "friends" to see exactly what you're up to at all times. Our time on Facebook has been a great learning experience. One thing we realized as we started out on our digital journey was that many of our close friends and family members didn't read our blogs until we started to make them accessible on Facebook. As a result, our biggest piece of advice with your personal page is that you update it with all of your blog postings.

To simplify the process, you can connect your Twitter feed through Facebook, allowing all of your friends to see your Twitter updates. If you're an avid tweeter, though, we wouldn't recommend this because the number of posts can get overwhelming for non-social media people.

Now let's talk Facebook fan pages. If you have a blog, we strongly, strongly suggest that you set up a Facebook fan page. Unlike personal pages, which limit you to 5,000 friends, fan pages allow you to have as many fans as possible. Allow this page to be a showpiece for your blog. The more you update, the more "likes" you will get.

Again, we suggest that anything you put on your blog—blog posts, videos, photos, press, etc.—goes on your Facebook fan page. In our experience, brands and companies are now using Facebook outreach as another component of their campaigns with bloggers. When we were spokespeople for T.J.Maxx/Marshall's Back-to-School, for example, we were asked to post everything on our Facebook pages. Brands and companies like to see a high number of "likes," and your ability to obtain them is another way for you to show your influence. We also suggest making sure that you update some personal stuff on your Facebook fan page, too. Allow people to feel connected and, to some degree, that they know you. Your blog is an extension of you, as are all other social media tools. Likewise, you can use your personal Facebook page and your Facebook fan page to give your network a sneak peek at your blog posts. You can also automatically link your blog feed to your Facebook page so that your posts publish directly to your own Facebook pages. People can conveniently read your thoughts and posts directly on Facebook while they are browsing online without needing to visit your website.

Generally, Facebook is a killer communication tool. If you post a status update that reads "just launched a blog called myartwillchangeyourlife.com," then all your Facebook friends will read this update and possibly visit your blog. The best thing about Facebook is that it aggregates people with common interests. For example, if you find one graduate from your high school, that person is likely connected to hundreds of other graduates of your high school. Similarly, your college, workplace, or small town may be connected through Facebook. This makes spreading a message quickly and virally very easy if you've done a good job connecting yourself through every channel you can think of (work, alumni, friends, family).

How to Get Started

Facebook is very easy to use. Head over to Facebook.com and set up an account, using the prompts. You may choose what photos you want to upload, what information you prefer to provide and to whom, what status updates you'd like to put out there, and which friends you want to "befriend." Facebook is extremely user-friendly.

Facebook Terminology

Like This option allows you to indicate your approval of someone else's post, or of a company or product you support. When you "like" a Facebook page, you will have full access to it going forward and will be able to see information exclusively available to people who have "liked" it. For example, Staples will give their Facebook fans information on product launches and exclusive deals. A note: When you "like" a blog or a person, make sure you have a reason why you're doing so. Otherwise, you won't create strong connections with the other fans.

Privacy While many people have expressed concern about privacy issues regarding Facebook, the company has made excellent strides in protecting its members. You have the ability to set your privacy settings for your account. Many moms worry about sharing photos and information that may be too much for the world at large to know. This is a valid concern, and you can easily go to the privacy setting and set up different settings for each person you're friends with. We recommend creating lists as a way to manage your various "buckets" of friends. Lists let you easily keep track of your closest friends, high school friends, college friends, neighbors, and professional acquaintances. You can sort and label these friends in any way you like, for your own convenient viewing and sharing. You can set the privacy settings for each group to the setting you're most comfortable with.

Wall Your wall is your canvas. This is where all status updates are housed and where your friends can comment back to your updates. Any update you make to your account will be added here, including when you become friends with someone new, add a video, comment on a friend's status, or change some element of your profile. This is your personal homepage on Facebook. A tip: just remember that every friend you allow to see your wall will see every message that is posted. Sometimes we see moms having long conversations with other moms on their walls; in that instance, using the private "message" function would be more appropriate.

Messages When you want to have a deeper conversation with one of your friends on Facebook, you send them a message. You can have a back-and-forth conversation while still viewing all of your past messages between the two of you. This is a much easier way to converse in a private setting.

Tag Whenever someone adds a photo or mentions you in a post, they have the option of "tagging" you. For example, when you are tagged, someone can look at a photo of you, and as they scroll over your photo, your name will appear. They also will be able to track back to your page. Our suggestion: whenever someone tags you, go to the photo/post and see if you want yourself tagged. One great thing about Facebook is that you can always untag photos. If someone tags you in a post, and you'd rather not be mentioned, ask that person to delete the tag.

Getting the Most Out of Facebook

To help you use Facebook to your advantage, here are some key lessons we've learned along the way:

- Just as every company needs a Facebook fan page, your online brand, blog, or business needs a page of its own.

- Use a Facebook page to support your brand and drive traffic to your website. You can use both your personal page and your business page for these purposes. To do this, create Facebook updates that lead back to your website.

- Consistently update your status, and comment on the status of others. "Updating our Facebook page is a way to speak to our customers without being too 'in your face' about it," says Nina Restirir, founder and owner of MomAgenda, a company that creates organizers designed with moms in mind. "We do giveaways, coupon codes, and just have conversations, and moms can join in or not. It's up to them."

- Don't overpromote yourself. The last thing people want to read about is your personal PR. It's great to celebrate your successes or mention your blog posts, but make sure to include other information, such as articles you find interesting and blogs you suggest. You could be unfriended fast if you only talk about yourself!

- Be well-rounded on Facebook. Share more than just your business face. You're a mom, a woman, maybe even a wife. Include all dimensions of your personality to create a likeable virtual you.

- One topic most moms agree on is that it's tough to balance it all, so try to engage conversation on that topic and others like it. Join groups like Social Media Moms. Start a group of moms online, and share ideas and tips and advice and contacts. Allow Facebook to be a virtual playground for you to connect, engage, and share.

YouTube

What It Is

YouTube is a very popular video-sharing website that features millions of videos. If you search by a topic or a name, you'll quickly see tons of related videos. Besides watching what's there, you can upload and share your own personal videos.

Why You Use It

A Digital Mom uses YouTube to gain more exposure and visibility. We post our YouTube videos—whether Audrey's mom fashion videos or Colleen's product review ones—weekly. As a result, we've been able to open ourselves to, and capture the attention of, a larger audience. With video content becoming more and more popular in the blogging world, YouTube has really become a blogger's new best friend because it's so easy to upload and embed videos.

How to Get Started

First, you need to have a video to share! Once you have that, head over to YouTube. com and create an account. We suggest making your account name the same as your blog name, so people can find your videos more easily.

Uploading is as simple as pressing the upload button, then selecting the video you want to upload. Once it's uploaded, you can go in, name your video, add a description, select a category that your video falls under, and tag it. Everything is prompted, so you won't have any trouble navigating these steps. We suggest naming your video something very searchable. "How to Wear a Scarf" is a good example because it's simple, straightforward, and likely to be typed in by someone as a search phrase. Naming that same video "Lots of Lovely Layers" sounds cute but will probably be missed by someone looking for specific instructions on how to wear a scarf. Once your upload is finished, it's out there for the world to see!

Getting the Most Out of YouTube

While there are many ways you can use YouTube to boost your digital career, here are five key things we recommend so you can get the most out of it:

1. Make sure you do some video response to other videos. Every YouTube video upload gives you the option to respond to someone else's video. The more responses you make, the more chances people will head over to check out your videos. It's a great way to gain YouTube traffic and visibility.

2. When you're tagging your videos, make sure you include as many tags as you can think of. The more tags you include, the better chances people will find your video.

3. If you're going to start adding video to your repertoire, make sure you upload to YouTube on a regular basis. The more videos you upload, the better your chances of getting more views.

4. Subscribe to other YouTube accounts. YouTube works very much like Twitter and Facebook—the more people you "friend," the more likely they are to friend you back.

5. Do some research on YouTube. Go to some of the videos that get millions and millions of hits. See what they're doing. Use them as a gauge to help you make your videos better.

LinkedIn

What It Is

LinkedIn is a fine way to expand your professional network. Your profile on LinkedIn is essentially an enhanced online résumé. Unlike Twitter, Facebook, and YouTube,

LinkedIn is 100 percent professionally based. The more connections and contacts you gather, the more powerful your business network becomes.

Why You Use It

LinkedIn is used to strengthen the network of professional contacts that will help you get ahead in business. If you're looking for more work, or if you're trying to get your content out into the world, share this information with your network. One thing we have learned—you never know who is lurking out there. Some of these contacts could potentially be game-changers for you.

How to Get Started

Head over to LinkedIn and create your account. As with all of the social media tools we have mentioned, sign-up is very user-friendly. Once you've created your account, start searching for past and present professional contacts, and begin linking to them.

Getting the Most Out of LinkedIn

As you connect with present and former colleagues, avoid trying to link with people whom you don't know and/or do not have any connections with. That's not the purpose of LinkedIn. Make sure to take your time in finding people to link to who know you and remember you.

Also, make sure you are constantly updating your profile. The life of a Digital Mom changes all the time as different opportunities present themselves. Make sure that someone who happens on your profile finds the most up-to-date summary of your professional accomplishments. You've already achieved them—now make sure everyone else knows about them.

KEY MOM BLOGS TO VISIT FOR INSPIRATION

Celebrity Gossip Blogs

Celebrity Baby Scoop: – www.celebritybabyscoop.com
Celebrity-Babies.com: – www.celebrity-babies.com
Famecrawler by Babble: – www.blogs.babble.com/famecrawler
I'm Not Obsessed: – www.imnotobsessed.com
MamaPop.com: – www.mamapop.com

Couponing Blogs

Common Sense with Money: www.commonsensewithmoney.com
Consumer Queen: www.consumerqueen.com
Coupon Cravings: www.couponcravings.com
Deal Seeking Mom: www.dealseekingmom.com
For the Mommas: www.forthemommas.com
Freebies 4 Mom: www.freebies4mom.com
Kingdom First Mom: www.kingdomfirstmom.com
Moms Need to Know: www.momsneedtoknow.com
Southern Savers: www.southernsavers.com
The Savings Lifestyle: www.savingslifestyle.com

Design Blogs

Baby Gadget: www.babygadget.net
Design Mom: www.designmom.com
Making it Lovely: www.makingitlovely.com
Morning T: www.morningt.blogspot.com
Oh Dee Doh: www.ohdeedoh.com

Project Nursery: www.projectnursery.com
Skimbaco Lifestyle: www.skimbacolifestyle.com

Entertaining and Arts & Crafts Blogs

Kids Kraft Weekly: www.kidscraftweekly.com
Makes and Takes: www.makesandtakes.com
Party Blue Prints: www.partybluprints.com
Woo Jr.: www.woojr.com

Fashion, Beauty, and Style Blogs

All Things Chic: www.allthingschic.net
Charmed Valerie: www.charmedvalerie.com
Chic Shopper Chick: www.chicshopperchick.com
LA Stylist Mom: www.lastylistmom.com
Mom Generations: www.momgenerations.com
MomTrends: www.momtrends.com
My Beauty Berry: www.mybeautyberry.com
Petit Elefant: www.petitelefant.com
Style Mom: www.stylemom.com
The Fashionable Housewife: www.thefashionablehousewife.com

Food Blogs

$5 Dinners: www.5dollardinners.com
A Southern Fairytale: www.asouthernfairytale.com
Cupcakes Take the Cake: www.cupcakestakethecake.blogspot.com
Food for My Family: www.foodformyfamily.com
Oh My Sugar High: www.ohmysugarhigh.com
Savor the Thyme: www.savorthethyme.com
Steamy Kitchen: www.steamykitchen.com
The Pioneer Woman Cooks: www.thepioneerwoman.com/cooking
My Wooden Spoon: www.mywoodenspoon.com
This Week for Dinner: www.thisweekfordinner.com
Two Peas and Their Pod: www.twopeasandtheirpod.com
Weelicious: www.weelicious.com

Green Blogs

Clean and Green Mom: www.cleanandgreenmom.org
Crunchy Domestic Goddess: www.crunchydomesticgoddess.com
Eco Child's Play: www.ecochildsplay.com

Gorgeously Green: www.gorgeouslygreen.com
MindfulMomma: www.mindfulmomma.typepad.com
Mommy Is Green: www.mommyisgreen.net
Non-toxic Kids: www.non-toxickids.net
SafeMama: www.safemama.com
The Green Mom Review: www.thegreenmomreview.com
The Smart Mama: www.thesmartmama.com
The Soft Landing: www.thesoftlanding.com
Zrecs: www.zrecs.blogspot.com

Mom Celebrities with Blogs We Love

Brooke Burke: www.modernmom.com
Denise Richards: www.deniserichards.com
Kourtney Kardashian: www.officialkourtneyk.celebuzz.com
Soleil Moon Frye: www.moonfrye.com

Photography Blogs

Moosh in Indy: www.mooshinindy.com
Secret Agent Mama: www.secretagentmama.com
Shutter Sisters: www.shuttersisters.com

Product Review Blogs for Moms and Children

A-List Mom: www.alistmom.com
Child Mode: www.childmode.com
Classy Mommy: www.classymommy.com
Cool Baby Kid: www.coolbabykid.com
Cool Mom Picks: www.coolmompicks.com
Cool Mom Tech: www.coolmomtech.com
The Divine Miss Mommy: www.thedivinemissmommy.com
Mamanista: www.mamanista.com
Mom's Favorite Stuff: www.momsfavoritestuff.com
MomFinds: www.momfinds.com
Mommies with Style: www.mommieswithstyle.com
Savvy Mommy: www.savvymommy.com

Travel (Near and Far) Mom Blogs

Globetrotting Mama: www.globetrottingmama.com
Guide to Military Travel: www.guidetomilitarytravel.com
Hip Travel Mama: www.hiptravelmama.com

Mommy Musings: www.mommymusings.com
Mommy Poppins: www.mommypoppins.com
NY City Mama: www.nycitymama.com
Theme Park Mom: www.themeparkmom.com
Travel Mamas: www.travelmamas.com
Traveling Mom: www.travelingmom.com
The Vacation Gals: www.thevacationgals.com
ZannaLand: www.zannaland.com

Miscellaneous Mom Blogs

Although it's impossible to list all the excellent mom blogs out there, here are some we love.

Adventures in Babywearing: www.adventuresinbabywearing.com
Amalah: www.amalah.com
Because I Said So: www.mom2my6pack.blogspot.com
Bizzie Mommy: www.bizziemommy.com
The Bloggess: www.thebloggess.com
Blonde Mom Blog: www.blondemomblog.com
Boston Mamas: www.bostonmamas.com
Carolina Mama: www.carolinamama1.blogspot.com
Cecily Kellogg: www.cecilykellogg.com
The Centsible Life: www.thecentsiblelife.com
Chicky Chicky Baby: www.chickychickybaby.blogspot.com
City Mama: www.citymama.typepad.com
Cool Mom: –www.coolmom.com
Cutie Booty Cakes: www.cutiebootycakes.blogspot.com
The Domestic Diva: www.thedomesticdiva.org
Dooce.com: www.dooce.com
Extraordinary Mommy: www.extraordinarymommy.com
Finslippy: www.finslippy.com
From Dates to Diapers: www.fromdatestodiapers.com
Frugal Upstate: www.frugalupstate.com
Girl's Gone Child: –www.girlsgonechild.net
Girlymama: www.girlymama.com
Go Graham Go: www.gograhamgo.com
Go Mom: www.gomominc.com
The Guilty Parent: www.theguiltyparent.com
Her Bad Mother: www.herbadmother.com
Home Ec 101: www.home-ec101.com
Hoo-Dee-Hoo: www.hoo-dee-hoo.com
I Should Be Folding Laundry: www.ishouldbefoldinglaundry.com
Jenny on the Spot: www.jennyonthespot.com

Jessica Gottlieb: www.jessicagottlieb.com
Ladies Live and Learn: www.ladiesliveandlearn.com
Lady and the Blog: www.ladyandtheblog.com
Lille Punkin: www.lillepunkin.com
Love That Max: www.lovethatmax.blogspot.com
Married My Sugar Daddy: www.marriedmysugardaddy.com
MckMama: www.mycharmingkids.net
Mocha Momma: www.mochamomma.com
Mom 101: www.mom-101.com
Mom Advice: www.momadvice.com
Mom Dot: www.momdot.com
Mom in the City: www.mominthecity.com
The Mom Salon: www.themomsalon.com
The Mom Slant: www.themomslant.com
The Mommy Blog: www.themommyblog.com
Momfluential: www.momfluential.net
Momma's Gone City: www.mommasgonecity.com
Mommy Brain Reports: www.mommybrainreports.com
Mommy Needs Coffee: www.mommyneedscoffee.com
Mommy Niri: www.mommyniri.com
Motherhood Uncensored: www.motherhooduncensored.net
Musings of a Housewife: www.musingsofahousewife.com
Nie Nie Dialogues: www.nieniedialogues.blogspot.com
NYT Motherlode: www.parenting.blogs.nytimes.com
Parent Hacks: www.parenthacks.com
Pundit Mom: www.punditmom.com
Queen of Spain: www.queenofspainblog.com
Real Mom Media: www.realmommedia.com
The Redneck Mommy: www.theredneckmommy.com
Resourceful Mommy: www.resourcefulmommy.com
Robyn's Online World: www.robynsonlineworld.com
Rock and Roll Mama: www.rockandrollmama.com
Role Mommy: www.rolemommy.com
Rookie Moms: www.rookiemoms.com
Scary Mommy: www.scarymommy.com
Simple Mom: www.simplemom.net
Socal Mom: www.socalmom.net
Sophistishe.com: www.sophistishe.com
Spanglish Baby: www.spanglishbaby.com
The Spohrs Are Multiplying: www.thespohrsaremultiplying.com
Stories from the Stoop: www.andrea-stanley.com
Storked!: www.glamour.com/sex-love-life/blogs/storked
Suburban Bliss: www.suburbanbliss.net
Suburban Turmoil: www.suburbanturmoil.blogspot.com
A Sundry Life: www.asundrylife.com

Sweetney: www.sweetney.com
Tech Mamas: www.techmamas.com
Tech Savvy Mama: www.techsavvymama.com
This Full House: www.thisfullhouse.com
Tip Junkie: www.tipjunkie.com
To Think Is to Create: www.tothinkistocreate.com
True Mom Confessions: www.truemomconfessions.com
Veep Veep: www.veepveep.com
Velveteen Mom: www.velveteenmom.com
Vodka Mom: www.vodkamom.com
Wholesome Mommy: www.wholesomemommy.com
Work It, Mom!: www.workitmom.com

Community Websites for Moms

Aiming Low: www.aiminglow.com
Alpha Mom: www.alphamom.com
AOL's Parent Dish www.parentdish.com
Babble: www.babble.com
BabyCenter: www.babycenter.com
Blissfully Domestic: www.blissfullydomestic.com
BlogHer: www.blogher.com
Cafe Mom: www.cafemom.com
Executive Moms: www.executivemoms.com
5 Minutes for Mom: www.5minutesformom.com
Hot Mom's Club: www.hotmomsclub.com
Lifetime Moms: www.lifetimemoms.com
Mom Bloggers Club: www.mombloggersclub.com
Mom Logic: www.momlogic.com
MOMocrats: www.momocrats.com
The Motherhood: www.themotherhood.com
My Gloss: www.mygloss.com
The SITS Girls: www.thesitsgirls.com
Theta Mom: www.thetamom.com
TODAY Moms: www.moms.today.com
Today's Mama: www.todaysmama.com
Type-A Parent: www.typeaparent.com

Appendix C

BUSINESS AND SOCIAL MEDIA RESOURCES FOR DIGITAL MOMS

BUSINESS

Books

The Big Idea: How to Make Your Entrepreneurial Dreams Come True, from the Aha Moment to Your First Million, by Donny Deutsch and Catherine Whitney

Getting to Yes: Negotiating Agreement Without Giving In, by Roger Fisher, William L. Ury, and Bruce Patton

Rework, by Jason Fried and David Heinemeier Hansson

The Girl's Guide to Starting Your Own Business, by Caitlin Friedman and Kimberly Yorio

The Tipping Point: How Little Things Can Make a Big Difference, by Malcolm Gladwell

Purple Cow: Transform Your Business by Being Remarkable, by Seth Godin

The Art of the Start: The Time-Tested, Battle-Hardened Guide for Anyone Starting Anything by Guy Kawasaki

The 12 Secrets of Highly Creative Women, by Gail McMeekin

The 10 Day MBA: A Step-by-Step Guide to Mastering the Skills Taught in America's Top Business Schools, by Steven Silbiger

Taxes

Internal Revenue Service (www.irs.gov): Find guidelines on tax regulations.

Legal

Disclosure policy (http://disclosurepolicy.org): Create a free disclosure policy for your blog, with custom html code, and add it to your site.Privacy policy (www.freeprivacypolicy.com): Create a free privacy policy for your blog, with custom html code, and add it to your site.

Federal Trade Commission (www.ftc.gov): Useful guidelines on how to disclose your sponsored content and posts.

Legal Zoom (www.legalzoom.com): Tons of free information on the legal aspects of running a business; a great resource for entrepreneurs.

Registering for an LLC

Biz Filings (www.bizfilings.com) and Legal Zoom (www.legalzoom.com): Go to these sites to register for your LLC.

Trademark, Patent, and Copyright Information

USPTO.com (www.uspto.com): Patents, trademarks, and copyrights; you can also do a trademark search here; not affiliated with the government.

General Information and Entrepreneurship

TheBusinessofBeingaMom (www.thebusinessofbeingamom): Website founded by a pair of mom entrepreneurs who invented BoogieWipes. They share all their experience and provide countless resources to those aspiring to become any style of mompreneur, from manufacturing tips to patent tips to blogging tips.

National Association of Women in Business (www.nawbo.org): A national professional association that represents the interests of women entrepreneurs through networking opportunities. You can join a local chapter to take advantage of their resources.

Entrepreneur (www.entrepreneur.com): The website for *Entrepreneur* magazine; excellent tips and articles for budding entrepreneurs.

Inc. (www.inc.com): The website for *Inc.* magazine, a publication for entrepreneurs and private business owners.

Working Mother (www.workingmother.com): The website for *Working Mother* magazine, which helps working moms find balance between work and family.

Make Mine a Million (www.makemineamillion.org): Organization dedicated to helping women grow their microbusinesses into million-dollar businesses.

Ladies Who Launch (www.ladieswholaunch): Provides resources for women in business and offers a networking organization.

85 Broads (www.85broads.com): An exclusive global business network, perfect for networking opportunities.

Funding

Visit any of these websites to get information on securing loans or funding to start or grow your business.

Women Owned (www.womanowned.com/growing/funding/opportunities.aspx).

Small Business Administration Office of Women's Business Ownership (www.sba.gov/aboutsba/sbaprograms/onlinewbc/index.html).

The Women's Funding Network (www.wfnet.org).

American Association of University Women (www.aauw.org).

SOCIAL MEDIA

Books

Mom 3.0: Marketing WITH Today's Mothers by Leveraging New Media & Technology, by Maria T. Bailey

Trust Agents, by Chris Brogan

Twitter Power 2.0: How to Dominate Your Market One Tweet at a Time, by Joel Comm

Blogging for Dummies, by Susannah Gardner

ProBlogger, by Darren Rowse and Chris Garrett

From Blog to Business, by Jennifer James and Esther Brady Crawford (a free e-book download: go to www.fromblogtobusiness.com/)

YouTube and Video Marketing: An Hour a Day, by Greg Jarboe and Suzie Reider

Mom Blogging for Dummies, by Wendy Piersall

Bloggertunity: A Mom's Guide to Blogging, by Stephanie Sheaffer (buy this e-book at www.metropolitanmama.net/ebook/)

The Yahoo! Style Guide: The Ultimate Sourcebook for Writing, Editing, and Facebook Marketing: An Hour a Day, by Chris Treadaway and Mari Smith

Crush It!: Why NOW Is the Time to Cash in on Your Passion, by Gary Vaynerchuk

Creating Content for the Digital World, by Yahoo!

Websites

Blogging Angels: www.bloggingangels.com

Blogging Basics 101: www.bloggingbasics101.com

Desperately Seeking WordPress: www.desperatelyseekingwordpress.com

Fast Company: www.fastcompany.com

Gizmodo: www.gizmodo.com

Mashable: www.mashable.com

ProBlogger: www.problogger.net

Savvy Blogging: www.savvyblogging.net

She Posts: www.sheposts.com

Tech Crunch: www.techcrunchcom

Wired: www.wired.com

Acknowledgments

First and foremost, thank you to the hundreds of Digital Moms who shared their insights and experiences with us to make this book possible. We're all in this together, and you inspire us every day. Thank you for all the encouragement, collaboration, and support. The online mom community is a marvelous place that continues to grow. We are so lucky to be a part of it.

From Audrey

To my four sons, William, Alexander, Benjamin, and Henry. If it wasn't for you boys, I wouldn't have become a Digital Mom. I love you so much. Everything I do is for you guys.

To my husband, Matthew. You've always dreamed the bigger dream with me. Thank you for holding my hand and being there throughout this whole journey. Most of all, thank you for believing in me. I love you crazy.

To my parents, Barry and Sharon Couto. Thank you for your endless (endless!) support since the very beginning, even when nobody really knew or understood what a "blog" was! Words cannot express how thankful I am for all that you have done for me, and how much you have always believed in me. I love you.

From Colleen

To Mike, Mackenzie, and Kyle. We are Classy Mommy. Thank you for your unconditional love, support, and encouragement. You are the reason that I was able to find a better way to live and work; you are why this book exists. Every day you make me live in the moment and appreciate life's simple pleasures. You taught me how to love, hug, snuggle, and giggle to a dream career at home. You are the keys that unlocked the corporate handcuffs and started the engine of my digital adventure. I love you all!

To my parents, Mike and Sharyn Costello, thank you for all your love, encouragement, and support over the years. I love you.

From both of us:

We would like to acknowledge some special people who made this book possible. To Danielle Svetcov, our literary agent. From the beginning, you understood our passion, our love, and our drive for this project. You recognized our strengths and the message we wanted to share with moms everywhere about the magical middle ground of being a Digital Mom. Thank you for all your hard work. Your efforts helped us make our dream a reality.

To Matt Inman, our first editor at HarperCollins. You saw something in this book that you felt was important to publish. You made us published authors and for that we cannot thank you enough. You immersed yourself into the world of mom-blogging, and we just love you for it! Your patience, dedication, advice, and hard work will never be forgotten. Thank you for believing in us.

To Cassie Jones, our current editor at HarperCollins, and Jessica Deputato, thank you for taking on this project at the final hour and seeing it to the end. We were lucky to be placed in such good hands.

Index